The Heart's Necessities

The Heart's Necessities

LIFE IN POETRY

Jane Tyson Clement
with Becca Stevens

Edited by Veery Huleatt

PLOUGH PUBLISHING HOUSE

Published by Plough Publishing House
Walden, New York
Robertsbridge, England
Elsmore, Australia
www.plough.com

ISBN: 978-0-87486-792-3

23 22 21 20 19   1 2 3 4 5 6 7 8

Cover photograph by Tabor Chichakly. Used by permission.

Library of Congress Cataloging-in-Publication Data

Names: Clement, Jane T., 1917-2000, author. | Stevens, Becca, author. |
  Huleatt, Veery, editor.
Title: The heart's necessities : life in poetry / Jane Tyson Clement with
  Becca Stevens ; edited by Veery Huleatt.
Description: Walden, New York : Plough Publishing House, [2019] | Includes
  index.
Identifiers: LCCN 2018061599 (print) | LCCN 2019004019 (ebook) | ISBN
  9780874868432 (epub) | ISBN 9780874868449 (mobi) | ISBN 9780874868456 (
  pdf) | ISBN 9780874860818 (pbk. : alk. paper)
Subjects: LCSH: Clement, Jane T., 1917-2000. | Clement, Jane T.,
  1917-2000--Criticism and interpretation. | Christian women--United
  States--Biography. | Women authors, American--Biography. | Christian
  biography. | Bruderhof Communities--United States--Biography. | Christian
  life--Poetry. | Christian poetry, American. | Christian poetry,
  American--History and criticism.
Classification: LCC PS3553.L3933 (ebook) | LCC PS3553.L3933 Z46 2019 (print)
  | DDC 811/.54 [B] --dc23
LC record available at https://lccn.loc.gov/2018061599

Printed in the United States of America

Contents

NOTE ON PHOTOGRAPHY

The ocean and outdoor photos in this book were
taken at Bay Head, New Jersey, by Tim Clement
(Jane Tyson Clement's son, pictured above),
October 2018.

The photos of Becca and her home in Brooklyn
were taken by Clare Stober, Richard Mommsen,
and Melinda Goodwin, October 2018.

The photos of Jane and her family are used
courtesy of the Clement family.

Editor's Note

T HERE'S MORE THAN ONE STORY HERE, and this little book contains several parts. First, selected poems by Jane Tyson Clement, presented more or less chronologically. In between the poetry I've sketched the details of Jane's life to give some context, and to make this remarkable woman's life available to those who love her remarkable words. But what makes it more than another biography or poetry collection is the interspersed commentary by Becca Stevens, a singer-songwriter who, decades later, is giving Jane's words new life even as the poems help her express the essence of her own art.

What could Jane and Becca have in common? As I worked with Becca on this book, the connections between these two women sometimes seemed too tenuous, the differences separating them all too concrete. What could Jane's life – a

Manhattan upbringing, Smith College, courtship and marriage in the midst of World War II, a home and a big family, and then the radical decision to join the Bruderhof community, a rag-tag bunch of Christian pacifists – possibly have to do with Becca, child of a musical North Carolina family raised on Bach and bluegrass, a graduate of the School of Jazz at the New School, a musician who has collaborated with the likes of David Crosby, Troy Miller, and Jacob Collier, based in Bed-Stuy, Brooklyn, but always on the go, taking her music all over the world?

But when I listened to these two artists, instead of looking at the particulars of their lives, a clear pattern began to emerge. The art of both women is a tribute to authenticity and personal integrity, the fruit of hard decisions taken to find and stay faithful to the truth about themselves and the world. In this book, and in Becca's music, you can hear them in conversation, and in harmony.

What are the heart's necessities? Jane and Becca both have far better answers than I, so I'll let them tell you. Or, I should say, if you let their art and their lives speak to you, they might guide you to answers of your own. I hope that through this book many others will hear and heed the wisdom in Jane's poetry and Becca's music and feel, with them, the divine discontent that moves us to love, to believe, to question, and to create.

Veery Huleatt
Walden, New York

Prelude

TWO YEARS AFTER THE PASSING of my dear friend and
musical collaborator Kenya Tillery, I was still struggling to find
the words to honor her life through song. I had tried many
times to write a song for Kenya, but the words I chose either fell
flat or seemed heavy-handed – rooted in sorrow rather than the
celebration of Kenya's life. She was passionate about bringing
people together to share and create, so it is easy to imagine her
smiling down the day I opened a book of poems by Jane Tyson
Clement and found the perfect words to finish her song. Kenya
would have treasured this book not only because of her deep
appreciation of artistic collaboration, but also because her love
planted the seeds that brought it all together.

KENYA WAS THE KIND OF PERSON who inspired everyone
fortunate enough to cross her path. Her infectious attitude

moved even chronic pessimists to see the preciousness of life. Thinking back, it's hard to believe I only knew her for about six months.

Kenya first reached out to me through Myspace, early in my career, announcing herself as my "biggest fan" and requesting my presence at her birthday bash in our hometown of Winston-Salem, North Carolina. We had many mutual friends, and her letter made me smile, so I called her to find out more.

On the phone, Kenya shared that it was her dream to celebrate an evening of performances by her favorite musicians with her family and closest friends. She offered to fly me home early for Christmas, so that we could spend a few days together in her home studio working on songs for the party and recording vocals for her upcoming album.

The conversation took a turn when Kenya said, "Full disclosure: I've recently undergone treatment for a relapse of breast cancer. I've lost my hair, and I'm sporting only half a pair up top, but I promise that what I lack, I make up for in determination and admiration!" She paused, and added, "I know this is a little intense, and I hope it won't deter you, but I completely understand if you choose not to come."

She apologized for not being able to pay more – she was using her savings and "extra money" from insurance for treatment to throw this party. Without hesitation I responded, "I'm in!" We stayed on the phone for hours, making a long list of our favorite songs, enthusing over our shared Elliott Smith obsession, and figuring out vocal parts she could sing on my originals. I distinctly remember feeling, the moment I hung up, that I had just found a long-lost sister.

Kenya had already been through treatment twice, and from our conversation I assumed that she was on the mend. But even at that point she must have had some premonition that her cancer would return. She had lost a great deal of time already, and wanted to enjoy the time she had left. I think that's why the party meant so much to her.

A few months later, we met at her home studio in the garage of her mother's house in Winston-Salem. When I pulled up, she came running out in a flowing white linen dress, grinning ear to ear, confidently owning her bald head and altered figure. We spent four days laughing, singing, writing music, and working on her album. Her songs were so strong both musically and lyrically, addressing her fears and drawing light from her struggles.

Kenya, 2004

We'd occasionally take "tea breaks," and it was during one of these that Kenya told me about her dreams. She yearned to take her music on the road and share it with the world, but she was held back by cancer, by having to stay close to home for treatments and rest, and by the fear of more cancer. She said she could speak to me in a way that she was reluctant to with her close friends and family because she felt so much guilt for putting them through this struggle for the second time.

Kenya's birthday bash was on January 26, 2008, and her friends and heroes flew in from all over the world. The event was a celebration of love and great music. Kenya was overjoyed.

The birthday bash: Becca (L) and Kenya

A few days later she made a guest appearance on one of my local gigs, singing for my friends and family, and I noticed her energy was down. Less than a week later, on the morning that I was scheduled to return to New York, she called me from the hospital. She'd had another relapse, but this time the cancer had spread much further than before. My dad and I rushed to the hospital so we could hug her before driving to the airport. I spoke to her on the phone a few more times after that, usually late at night when her spirits were down. I was convinced she would get through.

Kenya passed away on March 7, 2008. The invitation to her funeral came while I was out on tour. I was shocked by her death, and devastated that she didn't get more time to share her gifts. It felt unfair that I was missing her funeral while I was living the dream that she didn't get to fulfill. I promised then to honor Kenya by making the most of my time as a musician, and to keep her story alive by writing a song, a reminder of how lucky we are to still be here enjoying music, collaborating, and celebrating the lives of those we love.

EARLY VERSIONS OF THAT SONG were titled "Kenya's Song" but eventually it became "Tillery." For years, I would write a draft, demo it, decide it wasn't good enough for her, and put it away for six months to a year, before repeating the whole process. I was on the fourth rotation of this when I had the urge to pull a poetry book off my shelf for lyrical inspiration. I had settled on a theme about seasons and written a melody and lyrics about spring, but was searching for lyrics that would paint a picture of winter, touching on metaphors of loss without feeling too cold and dreary.

Jane Tyson Clement's *No One Can Stem the Tide* had languished unopened on my bookshelf for nearly a year, a neglected stocking stuffer my father had given me as an aid to unlocking inspiration in songwriting. Why hadn't I opened it sooner? Stubbornness, most likely, being stuck on the ideal of finding the perfect words myself. But for some reason, in that moment, the book caught my eye. I picked it up, thought of Kenya, and then opened to a random page. I was stunned to see two poems about winter side by side, titled "Winter" and "February Thaw." Not only did they capture the season of loss so perfectly, but they did so with exactly the right rhythm and number of syllables to fit the melody I had already written.

I immediately reached out to Jane's publisher and her surviving family to ask for the rights to pull phrases from those two poems to write a song. When they were so generous and accommodating, letting me use Jane's poems in whatever way would spread them to more people, I thought to myself: I'm definitely going to set more of her poems to music!

Now I have five:

- ▶ "Tillery"
- ▶ "105"
- ▶ "For You the Night Is Still"
- ▶ "Response to Criticism"
- ▶ "I Am No Artist"

Meanwhile, thanks to the power of Jane's words and Kenya's inspiration, "Tillery" has taken on a life of its own: it has been recorded on four different albums in four completely different settings, and has even become a band name.

MY FIVE JANE TYSON CLEMENT SETTINGS were written in various Brooklyn apartments during my years living in New York. Wherever it is, my home is my creative haven – a safe, quiet space where I can write when I'm off the road, reunited with my instruments and in control of my time.

Becca, 2018

An important part of my music-writing process is recording my ideas. I make home demos, using a lo-fi, homespun, DIY approach to recording. I then use the recordings to teach the songs to my bandmates, and finally send the demos to a producer who helps me craft and capture them in a professional recording studio.

I treasure these original home demos as time capsules that capture the essence of my original instincts, the unadulterated song at its core, before it was influenced by outside factors and opinions. I've often thought about making a whole record that way, foregoing the glossy perfectionist studio approach to embrace the more intimate and instinctive process, and to expose my deepest and truest sound.

When I learned that Jane, too, wrote from home, and that those who knew her thought of her as a teacher (and didn't even know she was a poet), I decided that this "Becca + Jane" collaboration was the perfect project to incorporate this homespun recording approach I have considered sharing for so long. The self-recorded audio of these five poetry settings led to five music videos filmed at my apartment in Brooklyn. (You can view these videos at *plough.com/jtc-songs*.)

THE TITLE OF THIS BOOK, *The Heart's Necessities*, comes from Jane's poem "Winter" (the first Jane poem I ever read, and a lyric in "Tillery"). Here is its original stanza:

> The heart's necessities
> include the interlude
> of frost-constricted peace
> on which the sun can brood.

I've often found it strange and beautiful that the heart aches when emotional elements are out of balance. When someone "breaks your heart," or when you miss someone, the chest grows heavy, the heart tugs and pulls. But these painful seasons are, to Jane, part of the necessity of being human, and without these periods of grief and "frost-constricted peace," the sun has no place to brood, to heal us, and to bring us back to springtime with the fruits of winter mourning.

Like Kenya, Jane wrote from the heart. Not because she was being hounded by a publisher or a record label, and not by any means to pay the bills. She wrote because it was her "heart's necessity." I hope that this heart-driven approach comes through in my recordings of Jane's poems, filmed and commissioned by the very people to whom Jane's poetry led me in January of 2011, almost exactly three years after Kenya's birthday bash.

I'VE ALWAYS GOTTEN THE SENSE that Jane was a strong, brave woman because her poems have a sensitivity that I've only ever found in the strongest people. She has a deep yet honest approach to sharing her emotional journeys, writing in a way that is universal yet personal. Jane also has a gutsy style, speaking her mind with class and without shame, and standing her ground even when admitting imperfection. I admire her deeply, even though we'll never meet outside the world of her poetry and stories.

No matter your beliefs or your struggle, you can find solace in Jane's words because she's woven them with a mastery that welcomes anyone. I often find myself returning to a poem I've read before and perceiving it in a completely new light due to a change in my own mood. This is the mark of a great artist: that she can write something as if she's speaking directly to you at a particular moment, and yet, with the same line, speak just as clearly to you in a different moment.

Since I first reached out to Plough in 2011, I have had the great pleasure of connecting with Jane's family members around the world. I've sung songs and shared meals with her son Tim (who took all the nature photographs in this book) and her granddaughter Anita, and relished hearing stories about Jane from the people who knew her well. I can't help thinking Kenya would get a kick out of seeing all these new connections and collaborations unfold as a result of her song.

My sincere hope is that this book will make the wisdom and beauty of Jane's life and poetry available to more people. I hope that my musical contributions will draw poetry enthusiasts to the music, and music enthusiasts to the poetry. I hope the backstory and commentary in this book will bring depth to the words that have added so much beauty to my life. Most of all, I hope Jane Tyson Clement's poems will bring the reader many years of solace and inspiration, just as they have done for me since the moment I read the first word.

Becca Stevens
Brooklyn, New York
November 2018

HORACE MANN AUDITORIUM

1935 Senior Class Play

FRIDAY EVENING
NOVEMBER 23, at 8:30 o'clock

Friday Evening
8:30 o'clock

Row L

Seat 21

REBA JANE TYSON
ELLEN EMERSON HOUSE
SMITH COLLEGE
NORTHAMPTON, MASS.

From the Sea

Gift

The sea will follow me through all my years,
Will lift mt heart in song, will quench my tears,
Will lay benignant hands upon my head,
At discontented whispers, sorrow led.

Death will find my body _____ it where
The ghastly shadows cr_____ ___ and sere,
Will choke my singing _____ _____ my eyes
To beauty which withi_____
The proofs of god, wh_____
Restored by gentle f_____

Yes, Death will fir_____
Who cling with ear_____
But not forever-no_____
The sea shall rai_____
My song again, re_____

Morning

I stood at the _____

With unbeliev_____
Lay an ocean _____
_____en running _____

_____ood at _____

Earth

(st)

You who have watched the wave_____
and heard the muted wh_____
shelter your heart with pati_____
and keep it free.

Let not the varied destru_____
urge to a lesser prize_____
keep faith with beauty now, and_____
stars you may shall find.

R.J.T.
March 10th 1938 — war coming

01

Shelter Your Heart with Patience

You who have watched the wings of darkness lifting
and heard the misted whisper of the sea,
shelter your heart with patience now, with patience,
and keep it free.

"Faith"

W HEN REBA JANE TYSON (known as Jane) won the poetry award on graduating from Horace Mann School in 1935, her father took the liberty of sending the prize poem, a lovelorn sonnet beginning "What trace of tears shall I now find . . ." to several of his colleagues at Columbia University. His pride is evident in the exclamation points that punctuate his observations, but is tempered with fatherly concern: "She's a queer mixture," he admits in one letter. "We're sure we have something in her, but she puzzles us sometimes with her maturity and this queer introspective touch."

His daughter was puzzled too. Who was Jane Tyson? The question occupied her throughout her early life. The outward details are simple enough to relate: two brothers, Jim older and David younger than herself, a middle-class upbringing near Columbia College, where her father held several administrative positions. The Tysons lived on Claremont Avenue, in the midst of New York's great educational institutions: Columbia, Barnard College, Julliard School of Music, Union Theological Seminary, International

House, and Horace Mann, which Jane attended from first grade through high school. Jane considered the beautiful Columbia campus her backyard, and spent hours playing there with her brothers. Her education included a good dose of New York culture: the Bronx zoo, operas at the Met, and hearing the New York Philharmonic perform under Arturo Toscanini. The family spent summers at their grandparents' farm in Pennsylvania, and later at Bay Head on the New Jersey coast, where the ocean seized Jane's heart and imagination. "The sea will follow me through all my years," she writes in an early poem, and it did: she would still be writing about it in the 1990s.

It was a sheltered childhood, but not completely. Jane was born in 1917, and the shadow of World War I hung over her early years: her father's closest friend had died in the trenches, and Jane, a sensitive child, observed the pain that war had caused her family and others. This seems to have been the foundation for her lifelong pacifism. Social causes were also close to her heart. Jane's father was a staunch Democrat – unusual in his milieu – and his father had been a lawyer who never made much because of his habit of representing coal miners and others who couldn't pay him in full. After the Wall Street Crash of 1929, when Jane was just eleven, she became accustomed to the sight of unemployed men on street corners, selling apples to passersby. Her mother never passed them without buying fruit, which Jane noticed and remembered.

As a teen, Jane became increasingly uncomfortable with the conventional Christianity she observed in the church her family attended. Churchgoers tolerated war, nationalism, racial inequality, and injustice, which Jane could not square with Jesus' teachings about love and peace, or with her own instincts about the preciousness of life. At seventeen, she announced to her father that she was an agnostic, and quietly stopped attending church.

But agnosticism was never a place to stay. It was a way of journeying, of admitting to herself and others that she was on a quest for truth. Jane never doubted that there was something out there far greater than herself. A juvenile poem begins:

I believe in some great god,
Some strange god of the sea,
A laughing god, a mocking god,
A god with peace in his arms,
A gift yet unbestowed.
A god of small moods,
A giver of insights too deep to be touched by words . . .

Her quest eventually brought her to Riverside Church, led by the famous pastor Harry Emerson Fosdick. Knowing that Fosdick was both a pacifist and deeply concerned about injustice, Jane worked up the courage to ask to meet with him. She remembered later: "I poured out my questions and doubts; he quietly listened and encouraged me to continue my search, to hold on to my belief in peace, and I would find what I was looking for, he was sure of that."

In the midst of all this, Jane's talent began to emerge in little poems about nature, her beliefs, creativity, and love. ("But don't worry," she noted in the margin of a lovesick poem sent to a friend, "I haven't depended on anyone so greatly as yet.") "Have I within myself found restless springs?" she asks in an early poem, and in another, "Why not lay down the power-less pen at last / admit defeat?" She was beginning to think of herself as a poet, but, despite the graduation prize, was also already doubting her creative abilities. "Take back my poet's soul. I cannot give / Its rich designs a worthy utterance. / Take back my soul, or give me poet's strength . . ." The restless springs of creativity and discontent were the source of new questions about the world, about God, and about herself.

High school graduation was soon followed by enrollment in Smith College, in the autumn of 1935. There Jane studied literature and poetry, taking classes with scholars like Charles Jarvis Hill and Howard Patch, and with the poet Grace Hazard Conkling. In 1936, she met the poet Archibald MacLeish, whose famous poem "Ars Poetica," (the art of poetry) she had probably read and taken to heart: "A poem should be equal to / Not true. . . . A poem should not mean / But be." Jane described their encounter in a poem of her own, "To Archibald MacLeish." While the actual meeting seems to have been a disappointment – "I touched his hand, but he will not remember" – it reveals Jane's new sense of self and purpose: "I aim to be a poet. That I have over him. / I aim at what he is. The fight is mine."

At times, her new self-confidence bordered on arrogance. In a letter home to her mother a few months later, Jane wrote: "You ought to get used to different styles of writing. For that reason I am sending home two books I think you would find helpful. . . . The Hemingway is rather warm and you probably won't like it but it is a good style to get used to, and a good kind of subject matter to get used to. If you shy away from that sort of thing you lose a lot." Smith College was transforming an introverted girl into a confident young woman.

Jane's heart was receiving an education as well. In a comparative religion class she encountered the writings of George Fox, the seventeenth-century reformer and founder of the Quakers (also known as the Society of Friends). No doubt Fox's vivid, almost poetic prose – "I saw, also, that there was an ocean of darkness and death; but an infinite ocean of light and love, which flowed over the ocean of darkness. In that also I saw the infinite love of God" – attracted her, but it was his honest, uncompromising search for "the faith which purifies and gives victory" that rang true to Jane, and she soon discovered, to her joy, that Quakers still existed – even on the Smith campus.

The Smith College chaplain, Burns Chalmers, was a Quaker, and he and his wife, Elizabeth, hosted open evenings for students. It was at their house that Jane met other students who were part of the peace movement, a loosely defined association that began as a reaction to the atrocities of World War I and continued to be active as a second world war threatened. Jane also began attending Quaker services in a small chapel in the college library.

During Jane's sophomore year, her father accepted the presidency of Muhlenberg College, in Allentown, Pennsylvania, and the family moved there, away from the Manhattan home of Jane's childhood. During her senior year, Jane decided to pursue teaching and applied for several positions. Through her new Quaker connections, she was accepted for a teaching internship at Germantown Friends School, at the edge of Philadelphia.

College graduation, like high school commencement four years before, brought with it a literary prize. For her long narrative poem, *Strange Dominion*, Jane won the Mary Augusta Jordan Prize, awarded for the "best original literary work" of the graduating class. The final six poems in this chapter are taken from *Strange Dominion* – where they are like interludes that break up the blank verse of the narrative. A friend with connections in the publishing world sent the manuscript off to Macmillan while Jane, after a summer at Bay Head, was off to teach school.

GIFT

The sea will follow me through all my years,
will lift my heart in song,
will quench my tears,
will lay benignant hands upon my head
at discontented whispers, sorrow led.
Death will find my body, hide it where
the ghastly shadows creep, all brown and sere;
will choke my singing voice,
will blind my eyes
to beauty which within the seasons lies,
the proofs of God, which fade and rise again,
restored by gentle fingers of His rain.
Yes, Death will find me.
Not immortal, I
who cling with earth-stained fingers
also die –
but not forever – no.
The sea will raise my song again,
remembering all my praise.

1935
Bay Head, New Jersey

Becca: When I was growing up, my family spent summer vacations at a beach house in Hilton Head, South Carolina. Melodies and lyrics would come to mind seamlessly there while I walked the length of the beach, searching for pretty shells and sharks' teeth, and gazing out at the changing colors on the ocean. Several of my songs are a direct result of these solo walks, churning struggles into song, lulled and comforted by the waves, the seagulls, the feeling of the sand, and the ocean's vast peace. The beach house is gone now but my relationship to the ocean remains.

Jane used to spend time with her family in Bay Head, New Jersey. She knew the sea as an earthly mother, lifting her heart in song and easing her sorrows. But for Jane, the ocean also represents an eternal place where her creations live on after she is gone, raising her song and remembering her praise.

This is one of those poems that seems to miraculously apply to whatever struggle I'm going through as I'm reading it. The death she mentions could be the end of her life, or perhaps the death of creativity, love, or faith. This death could also be Jane's doubt, or the dark cloud of depression that comes with such doubt, "blinding our eyes to the beauty."

But in this poem, the sea is stronger than death, doubt, depression, and all the things that go hand in hand with our mortality. The sea represents art in its truest form.

THE ALIEN LAND

Never before saw I trees leaning on the sky,
Green-sharpness cutting through the endless blue.
I am a seachild, used to wind that makes
Music of its own, not of the leaves.
Never before saw I the hermit birds that fly
Low in the quiet shade where tall trees made
The forest floor grow bare and needle-brown
Always the birds I love hang in the wind above,
crying their pain over the ruffled sea.
Never the sweet lament, never the soft content
the robin whistles from the swaying elm.
I am the sea's lone child, loving the sky's sea-wild
And windy limits where the gull's flight ends.

1937
Smith College
Northampton, Massachusetts

TO ARCHIBALD MACLEISH

I touched his hand, but he will not remember.

I looked into his eyes, tea-colored,
and he smiled at me,
not knowing who I was or caring
other than that I was young and just beginning.
He did not know that I stood then
where he once stood,
or that I wanted what he now had found;
will and power of words.
He lays his thoughts
clearly like jewels flashing in the light,
simple, unset except with what the mind
must have to shape itself.

I touched his hand, but he will not remember.

I aim to be a poet. That I have over him.
I aim at what he is. The fight is mine.
He looked as though he knew once what it meant
and had not quite forgotten.

I touched his hand, but he will not remember.

October 15, 1936
Smith College

Becca: I relate to this poem from the perspective of both characters: the fan – idealizing the hero, hoping to be recognized for her adoration, and the artist – maybe tired from having just finished performing, failing to satisfy the admirer's wish to connect in a meaningful way.

I picture Jane here, barely nineteen years old, a college student pondering an anticlimactic interaction with her poetry hero. Sometimes I read this poem and project my own memories of disappointing interactions with musicians whose art has inspired mine, but on closer inspection I notice that Jane never mentions disappointment or resentment. Even in her teens, she had the insight to recognize the interaction for what it was, and the confidence to claim her inexperience and her "fight" to be a poet as strengths.

MacLeish would have been forty-five years old at that time, a politically active anti-fascist working as a writer and editor for *Fortune* magazine, having already won his first of three Pulitzers. In his early twenties, MacLeish's studies at Harvard Law School had been interrupted by World War I, in which he drove an ambulance and served as an artillery officer. His brother was killed in action during the war. (It's possible that his anti-war poems, like *Memorial Rain*, also influenced Jane's pacifism.)

I imagine MacLeish, a worn down, world-renowned poet finishing up a college seminar, the students politely lined up to shake his hand, and Jane standing proudly at the front of the line. MacLeish offers a handshake and quick smile to a sweet young girl whose eyes are full of familiar admiration. Maybe he sees something of himself as a young poet for a flash, and then he is on to the next handshake.

This poem serves as a reminder to always maintain presence and humility when meeting someone who approaches in admiration, because in the end, we are all students together. The greatest artists and teachers consider themselves students until the end. Succumbing to the idea that you've "made it" and that you have nothing left to learn is death to your art. David Crosby is one such artistic "reacher" and hero of mine: at seventy-seven he is touring with new projects, writing with new people, and pushing himself. As a result he is happier and more humble than he has ever been.

"The fight is mine" is my favorite line in this poem. The "fight" – reaching beyond your comfort zone, searching for new terrain and stumbling into the unknown – is one of the most important parts of being an artist and a human being.

FIRST SNOW

I felt it coming in the thin, blue air.
I saw it in the sky, delaying there,
divinely punctual, for the secret nod
and signal for descent from some snow-god.

I should have known the clouds would waver down
slowly, until they lay upon the ground
and we could walk, feet kicking up the sky
beneath, that once was hanging white and high.

I should have been prepared for this new sight
of something moving downward in the night,
of snow-flame creeping outward on the trees,
and gathering on the roofs, along the eaves,

ticking against the window, flickering by,
or landing on the ledge to melt and die,
holding its pattern for one little space
of time against the wood like fragile lace.

I covered up the flower beds to prepare
for what I knew was near, yet unaware
I let the white drift downward in the still
cold air, to find defeat upon my sill.

1938
Smith College

FOREBODING

Across the shallows tawny shadows run
and one grey osprey circles in the sun
over the still, green sea. The moment rests
hot on the sands and on the sunwhite dunes;
the moment is perfection, with the slow
draw of the waves, the gliding of the bird
lonely and silent in the empty air.

It will not last: the osprey will wing off
into the West, the tide will turn, the sky
pile up the clouds, the great grey shadows run
across the sands and shut away the sun.

April 15, 1937
Bay Head

SUMMER NIGHT STORM

The ranting of the gods, this tumbling sky,
this wind-strong rain which pelts against my cheek,
the world re-lit by lightning, and the lie
of tall sea grass low bent against the sand.

I stand here, strangely still, with all the world
tumultuous at my feet, and yet my heart
is stronger than the roaring wind that swirls
about my body, taut against its force;
that blows my eyelids shut, that locks my lips,
lest all my spirit end its restlessness
in one wild song.

c. 1938
Bay Head

THE BRASS LOCUST

So now again the tide wanes and the air
is rich with what would rather be forgotten;
and hard on the moving, on the changing wind
the eternal locust sounds its sharp despair:

the rasp of autumn and the rasp of heat,
metal of prophecy but not of peace,
awl in the ear to make us bondsmen here,
brand in the flesh of mind; under the beat

of sun, of light rain, of the dazzling earth
we lose the visioned, the encompassing eye;
the brass of locust boring in the noon
speaks for the alien and the coming dearth:

the unwise lift their heads, remembering cold,
regathering wisdom, as the sun grows old.

July 31, 1938
Sherman, Connecticut

HOW CAN WE HEAR

How can we hear
the sound of wind
within the rain,
though wind is still?
How can we see
the look of dusk
upon the hill,
though it be day?

Rain is not rain
alone; nor day
completely day;
nor is the earth
solely of earth –
and in the mind
one finds the heart –
and in the seed
death holds a part.

July 1938
Sherman

FAITH

You who have watched the wings of darkness lifting
and heard the misted whisper of the sea,
shelter your heart with patience now, with patience,
and keep it free.

Let not the voiced destruction and the tumult
urge to a lesser prize your turning mind;
keep faith with beauty now, and in the ending
stars you may find.

March 10, 1938
Smith College
"war coming"

I WAIT NO DESTINY

I wait no destiny, I am convinced;
I stir no hands, I light no eyes from mine,
nor will my music ever shake the stars,
my words turn years to leaves before the wind.

I am the listener always, and no more;
I take my light from others, and my hands
move at another's bidding, and my voice
echoes the words I cannot claim my own.

Oh, but I share the consciousness of breath;
I have my purpose – I fulfill my days.
Somewhere within me is the invulnerable flame
which hissed and flared the day man first took fire
and stirred and woke, and knew his first desire.

c. 1938
Smith College

IT IS TOO LATE

It is too late; you made me wait too long,
held my heart ringed with fire until the spell
broke and the flames were quieted to dust,
and I need wait no longer for your horn
sounding among the hills. I would be wise
to walk forgetting in this new release,
to give my free hands to this world's demand,
God's will – or the will of righteousness on earth –
too long was I apart from the needs of men,
single-starred and waiting, deep in sleep.

But lo, I rise and blow upon the ashes,
brush them aside, and seek the farthest hill,
calling your name and asking of your passage.
I am not free – I wait upon you still.

January 24, 1939
Smith College

THE SEA IS DUSK NOW

The sea is dusk now, and the wind is dying;
landward the last night-driven gull is flying.
Give up your mind now to the destined dark
and under the wide sky arched and high with stars
seek not the daylight and the touch of sun.
Accept the strong design – unlimited
by light, by dark, by wind and slow stars creeping:
there is a deep heart which is never sleeping!

February 25, 1939
Smith College
"in the infirmary recovering from pneumonia"

Becca: Jane wrote this poem when she was twenty-two, recovering from pneumonia in the infirmary at Smith College. Pneumonia was a big deal at the time, still the leading infectious cause of death in the United States throughout the 1930s.

I imagine Jane's return to writing after a period of fevers, painful coughs, and fatigue. The opening lines of the poem, "The sea is dusk now, and the wind is dying: / landward the last night-driven gull is flying," suggest the calm just after a heavy storm has passed. In this moment of gathering darkness Jane is surrendering to the night, and trusting that she will greet the morning. The poem's ending is deeply spiritual, accepting and embracing the faith that the "strong design" – destiny, or God's will – is greater than the coming night, and ultimately "unlimited by light, by dark, by wind and slow stars creeping."

"The destined dark": that phrase reminds me of the "necessary evil" from Jane's poem that begins "There are things to be remembered" (which I set to music in my song "105"). Both of these lines represent things we fear that, once accepted, bring us strength and meaning.

Within that "destined dark" is the heart that never sleeps. Maybe that "deep heart" is the sea of creative energies beneath the "wide sky arched and high with stars." Maybe the "deep heart which is never sleeping" is God, or the spirit deep within the artist.

Into the dark which is not dark
but only the light we cannot see,
reluctantly I let you go.
What was your source – children of years?
Surely I cannot claim your birth;
for when I found you, even then
you were not strangers to the earth.

I was the privileged, to disclose
briefly, a portion of your days.
Now you are free – but not complete;
for none of us is this the end.
Somewhere the valley holds the mist,
the four fields shimmer in the haze,
the man of patience and the child
and the sea-eyed girl draw deep their breath
and live, and have no fear of death.

April 1939
Smith College

Becca: When I first read this poem, I thought Jane was mourning the loss of a child, but after reading more about Jane's life, I discovered that Jane is addressing characters from her narrative poem *Strange Dominion*.

I often liken the relationship of an artist to her creations to that of a mother to her child. This dynamic rings true for me especially when making a record:

1. The writing period: deeply personal and internal, a long introspective phase like a pregnancy, intimately considering every word and every note to build each song perfectly.

2. The recording period: exhausting, terrifying, exciting, and surprising (not unlike raising a tiny human). Hearing sounds that only ever lived inside the mind finally spring to life! Hearing melodies rise up to their potential and interact with other sounds you never imagined. Even with a clear plan, the recording process never goes as expected. This phase is often collaborative, and that transition to sharing – with a producer, engineers, and other musicians – can be scary. What if the collaborators take the songs too far away from your original vision? Even if they do miss the mark, the process of loosening your grip allows for growth and strengthens the vision.

3. The post-production period: this phase is a lot of organizing and planning. I like to be very involved in the editing and mixing process because I want to know everything

that goes into the soup, and also because it helps me say goodbye. I often drag my feet a little at this point, fixating on tiny last-minute changes rather than realizing it's time to set it free.

4. The album release: The record is finished, all the arrangements have been made, and there's this surreal moment when you have to let go of the thing that has been so close to you for so long, consuming all your time and energy, like sending your kindergartener off for the first day of school.

In this poem, I think Jane is moving through this vulnerable moment of setting her creation free. Deciding that your creation is complete means it's no longer in your control. That can be unsettling, but if you want your hard work to live on beyond yourself, you have to share it. Only then is it free to move through others, to grow, inspire, and live a life of its own.

I'm touched by the gratefulness with which Jane bids farewell to her muses, implying that she was a mere vessel fortunate enough to "disclose briefly, a portion of [their] days." Jane asks about their "source," a question many great artists have pondered, implying that her art doesn't come from her, it comes from beyond. "Surely I cannot claim your birth; / for when I found you, even then / you were not strangers to the earth." This reminds me again of the vast sea of creativity artists draw from. Our creations exist there eternally, "and have no fear of death." At our best, we are out of the way, making room for the "light we cannot see" to pour in, paving the way for the muse, ancient and eternal, to stop in for a moment and move through us.

BETWEEN US LIE THE WATERS

Between us lie the waters, dark and still;
for all our love, the sea will lie between;
for all our passion, which will surge and fill
the heart to breaking; and for all the clean-
stripped honest words of truth we speak;
still will those level depths, unchanged, serene,
deny us the last union which we seek;
and in the end we must accept despair,
knowing that what we breathe is mortal air.

July 1, 1939
Bay Head

TELL ME IT IS ENOUGH

Tell me it is enough to be as I am now,
    and young,
and filled with the dark necessity of you,
and with delight at the thin crying of a gull
    against sunlight and bright water.

Tell me it is enough,
that more is not required of me,
that I need not stain my hands with the
    world's blood
or choose which side to hate,
or give up this drift of my heart, this joy,
this insupportable joy at the gull's white cry
and your hand lifted to me.

Tell me I must not deny my life,
    for the world,
for the world's hate and the world's anger.

July 24, 1939
Bay Head

I AM NO ARTIST ▶

(No true desire burns within me now.
I am no artist, lonely and supreme,
fulfilled within myself, needing no hand
to touch, no eyes to smile, no lips to speak.)

The wind roars in the pines and I am sad,
wanting your presence here. The blue jay flies
over the ruffling water to the hill,
lonely and dark and scattered yet with leaves.
I'd ask you why this bird will never go
south when the prophesying geese honk past
into a sunny heaven. Why stay here
where snow blinds and the icy dawn is still,
when there are strong blue wings to bear you out
into a wide sky, into a singing land?
I'd ask you that and wait for your reply,
knowing your wisdom must exceed my own.

(The wind roars in the pines and I am sad,
wanting you here beside me. Now I know
I am no artist, lonely and supreme,
needing no hand to touch, no eyes to smile.
Only your lips, your presence here, would seem
to send me winging southward mile on mile.)

c. 1939
Smith College

▶ This icon marks the poems put to music by Becca.
   They can be listened to at *plough.com/jtc-songs*

Becca: I adore this poem; I knew I wanted to do a setting of it from the moment I read the title. When I first read through the poem, I pictured Jane at the end of her life, looking out on the sea that had brought her so much poetry, now not enough to ease her human desires like longing for the presence of a loved one who's not there. When I found out that Jane actually wrote this poem when she was only twenty-one or twenty-two, I was shocked.

As a touring musician, I spend a lot of time apart from my husband (who's also a touring musician). We both struggle with being far away from each other and from our home, and this can take a toll on our focus as artists. A common misconception about touring artists is that our lives are fun and we should have a superhuman amount of physical and emotional strength to perform our best show, every show. The reality is that the touring musician's lifestyle can be pretty brutal. There's no grounding, no predictability, little routine, heavy bags, too many airports, and not enough sleep. Even though there's very little alone time on the road, somehow it is on the road that I feel the most alone.

This poem sounds almost like Jane is reacting to someone who had her pegged all wrong. Perhaps someone had assumed she was the "artist type": self-fulfilled, self-serving, and not needing a partner to share her life. But Jane makes it clear that

she does not see herself as such. She was a strong woman with weaknesses, insecurities, and the human desire to love and be loved.

Jane is speaking to someone she longs to be close to, to feel the comfort of their presence, and to trust that person to know the answers to her innermost questions. I think she is the bird that "will never go south," and even though she has the "strong blue wings" to bear her out into "a singing land," she doesn't feel she can make this journey on her own; she longs for the presence of a loved one to lift her out of the wintry sadness and send her "winging southward."

I imagine her trying to write, feeling distracted by loneliness and crippled by her own internal criticisms: "I'm nothing. I am no artist. I don't know the answers." Jane is struggling to create when pieces of herself are missing, but by expressing that vulnerability she creates beautiful art.

BACH INVENTION

If I could live as finished as this phrase,
no note too strong; each cadence purposed, clear,
the logic of the changing harmony
building and breaking to a major chord
strangely at home within a minor web
of music; if I could define my end,
from the beginning measures trace my course,
I might be old and prudent, shown by laws
how to devise a pattern for my days
and still be free, unhampered, yet refined.

He sat before the keys and turned the notes
into a fabric of design and peace;
here are the notes, the keys, my fingers free
to run them through their course, and here my mind
seeing his wisdom work within the chords,
finding his knowledge in the finished line.
I would be wise if such restraint were mine.

1939
Smith College

Becca: I stand behind every word of this poem! Bach's music takes my breath away, gathers my focus with its dancing lines, and inspires me with its intricacy, confidence, and sensitivity. Three centuries after his death, Bach's voice is still like no other, and his music is as inspiring as the day he first "sat before the keys and turned the notes / into a fabric of design and peace."

Bach is my desert island composer. His compositions are spiritual, perfect, complex yet direct, meditative, and, even after thousands of listens, they never cease to reveal something new. I love Jane's idea of life like a Bach phrase, "no note too strong; each cadence purposed, clear . . . at home within a minor web," embodying the balance of restraint and freedom in Bach's writing.

I picture a twenty-two-year-old Jane at the piano, playing through a Bach invention, moved to peace and poetic inspiration by the musical fabric, and admiring the restraint and maturity with which it was woven.

I relate to Jane's sentiment here: "I would be wise if such restraint were mine," especially when I read her poetry. Jane exemplifies that restraint, but the fact that she doesn't recognize it in herself makes her that much more beautiful as an artist, always reaching and seeing her own potential beyond her grasp.

When I was in my late teens (around the same age Jane was when she wrote "Bach Invention"), I was moved to write a poem inspired by the seventh of Bach's *Goldberg Variations*. Several years later I composed a choral arrangement setting of that poem, commissioned by the Melodia Women's Choir of New York City. Here's that poem:

Soli Deo Gloria

When that first note is flung into stillness
So begins a perfect minute and sixteen seconds
Brilliant & resolute

A breathless instant I await;
the first roulade sung so light and sweet
Like drops of water thrown effortlessly
From the wings of a bird

As the cadence subtly slows I know
I am leaving a perfect moment in time, by and by
Which will without fail
Be followed by a strange awareness of my every hair and then
Silence
The gift of this music is forever
Fresh in my mind like a secret

Soli Deo Gloria means "To God alone be the glory." Bach sometimes put the initials SDG at the end of his works to indicate where the attention should be. While the *Goldberg Variations* were not church music, they touch me, as does all of Bach's music, on a divine and spiritual level, as if the music is a connection between human listeners and God.

OH FAULTLESS DARK

Oh faultless dark and final night of peace,
why is there fear possessing all my bones,
warm in my blood and quivering in my eyes?
Must all the heart's assurance sometime cease,
or is it not the certain past atones
the future's doubt? No, see, the old faith dies
and flickers out like stars before the rain,
and all the years of certainty are worn
ghosts of an early and forgotten morn,
powerless to stir the wind of dawn again.

1939
from Strange Dominion
Smith College

DARK INTERVAL

You were a music once, beyond my fingers
beyond the keys man makes and plays upon;
the sweet chorale is finished and is ended;
the harmony has risen and has gone
into the mind of God where it will linger
always among all beauty we have lost.
Here there is silence sudden and profound;
here I call out, the hollow echo answers;
no cool thrush speaks of evening from the thickets
within the white drugged tautness of the noon;
there is no upward rush of your bright song:
only this lack of melody, this deep,
dark interval too empty and too long.

1939
from Strange Dominion

Mother of sorrows, look upon me now.
There is a heart within my heart, and eyes
within my eyes; oh, say upon my brow
some measure of your certain blessing lies.
Soon enough this pulse will beat alone,
new and unsure within a stranger land,
sharing the exile of our flesh and bone,
watching for sign of some uplifted Hand.
Grant me your grace now to be unafraid,
instill within me music and some peace
so that upon the child there will be laid
already joy before it seeks release,
so that its share of breath is full of light
and will be rich and strong before the night.

1939
from Strange Dominion

Becca: This poem feels akin to Shakespeare's sonnets, not just in its structure, but also in its self-reflective, longing nature.

In *Strange Dominion,* this poem is spoken by a character who is expecting a child, but it's so personal that I can't help wondering if it expresses something Jane herself was going through. Perhaps "Mother of sorrows" is Mother Mary, and the "heart within my heart, and eyes within my eyes" is Jane's faith in Jesus, which she struggled with during her formative years. Or maybe Jane is the mother, directing the prayer to her muse, or to the characters themselves, asking to be granted new inspiration once she has released her finished creations.

Jane has a rare ability to talk about God, spirituality, and faith in a way that anyone can relate to – not in an alienating way. She may be speaking about her faith, but the reader can understand it as something completely his or her own. I have an open mind when it comes to religion and spirituality, but I tend to shy away when things get too dogmatic – or really any time a person or group of people claim to know everything. Jane uses imagery rooted in nature to illustrate the inexplicable beauty of God. She looks to the movements of birds, the sea, and the seasons to answer her unresolved struggles with faith. This way of speaking to her God is a gift to everyone, because people of any faith, or even of no faith, can draw strength and truth and inspiration from her poetry.

NOW THAT MY LOVE HAS COME

Now that my love has come I see the reason;
now I answer its demand;
it was here always just beyond my vision
waiting for your lifted hand.

It has the width of sea, the depth of shadow;
it holds the storm wind wild and strong,
and light drawn thin to stars in the sweep of heaven
and the prow's clear water-cleaving song.

1939
from Strange Dominion

For you the night is still;
the moonlight on the hill
shall come no more. And I
whose life was touched with flame,
if I stay not the same
because the flame must die,
you will not know.

For me the night will change,
the moonlight not be strange,
nor silvered hill. And you
whose life was turned to dark
sleep on and do not mark
if this small heart stay true,
if love will go.

It is for me to keep
the beauty, while you sleep
unsullied peace. And I
who cannot stay the years
nor live them all in tears
must watch the vision die
unchecked and slow.

1939
from Strange Dominion

Becca: I first came across this poem while actively looking for one to set to music for this project. As I was reading it, the melody started to emerge naturally from the hypnotic words and the lull of the six-syllable iambic rhythm. I was drawn to the trotting pattern of the accents, the singable quality of the words, and the poem's artfully repetitive structure. In short, it felt like a song lyric already.

I find the enjambment at the end of the third line of each stanza intriguing so I accentuated it in the melody, creating a brief pause where the song seems to float in midair, before continuing on like a feather in the breeze.

The symmetrical yet serpentine nature of this lyric led to a single-note melodic cycle in the charango accompaniment (the Peruvian instrument I play on this song) that is almost medieval in style, which in turn inspired a haunting cyclical melody for the voice. The suspense of the spaces in the poetry is heightened with a "shimmer" reverb on the charango, and then accompanied by swells of wordless vocals.

I wrote my setting for this poem around the same time as "I Am No Artist," imagining both poems coming from an older Jane, perhaps after the passing of her husband, Bob. I sang these words over and over again with a very clear picture in my mind of what I thought was going on. When I learned that Jane wrote this poem before she met Bob, I felt as if I was discovering it again for the first time!

"For you the night is still." Who is the "you"? It's a riddle to me. Is she speaking to the moon? To God? To a college crush? The mystique is more important than my projected answer. I'm happy to leave it unsolved, or better yet, to arrive at a different answer every time I sing it.

Here, on this surge of hill, I find myself
not as I am or will be or once was,
not as the measure of days defines my soul;
beyond all that a being of breath and bone,
partaker of wind and sun and air and earth,
I stand on the surge of hill and know myself.
Below, the stars sink landward, and above
I breathe with their slow glimmer; fields are gone,
the woods are fallen into the speechless dark;
no claim, no voice, no motion, no demand.

It is alone we end then and alone
we go, creatures of solitary light;
the finger of truth is laid upon my heart:
See and be wise and unafraid, a part
of stars and earth-wind and the deepening night.

1939
from Strange Dominion

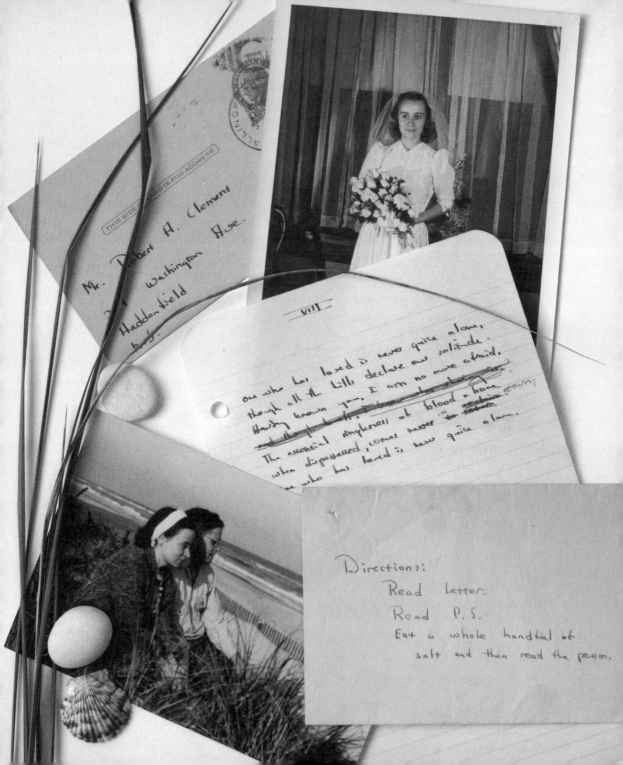

Mr. Robert H. Clement
___ Washington Ave.
Haddonfield
N.J.

THIS SIDE OF CARD IS FOR ADDRESS

VIII

one who has loved is never quite alone,
though all the hills declare our solitude.
Having known you, I am no more afraid,
~~and the help thereof the seal~~ ...
The essential singleness of blood & bone
when dispossessed, comes never to return;
one who has loved is never quite alone.

Directions:
Read letter.
Read P.S.
Eat a whole handful of
salt and then read the poem.

02

One Who Has Loved
Is Never Quite Alone

One who has loved is never quite alone,
though all the hills declare our solitude.

"To R.A.C. VIII"

J ANE MET ROBERT ALLEN CLEMENT, "Bob" to family and friends, in September 1939, just before classes began at Germantown Friends School. As she was on her way to a staff mixer, a cheerful young man caught up with her, introducing himself as Bob Clement. When Jane introduced herself, he said, "Oh, so you're the college president's daughter." Jane was nettled by this, and remembered years later, "I had wanted to be known for myself, not for any position my father had. I thought he was a bit tactless and nosy, but he had a likeable face, so I cheerfully said that I was, so what!"

Bob, Jane discovered, was a lawyer's son, the only child of a Quaker couple from Haddonfield, New Jersey. He was midway through law school but, because he had always been interested in education, was taking a year off from his studies to teach.

The interns at GFS got to know each other well. Most were pacifists, so Jane at last found herself in an environment where she was not alone in her beliefs. It's hard to know when Bob began to stand out to her, but in November 1939 she wrote her first poem dedicated to him, detailing a chance encounter in the school library: "You entered, and I know you saw me there; / by all the stars above I swear / my heart was calling so you must have heard." He did not seem to hear it, and the poem ends:

> I watched the door swing to, and heard it latch –
> and knew we two were not a match,
> and went back to my reading, and forgot
> the things we were to be, and now were not.

In the face of Bob's indifference, Jane tried to school herself in acceptance, enjoying his friendship and, in the meantime, going out with other young men.

But patience proved harder after an evening spent together in April 1940. Bob had asked Jane out, and, as he was walking her home after dinner, she felt sure that he was the one for her. But she had no reason to believe that he felt the same way toward her. Their chances of seeing each other were curtailed by the end of the school year, after which Bob would return to law school and to helping at his father's law firm; Jane, after the summer in Allentown and at Bay Head, would take up a teaching position at the Shippen School for Girls in Lancaster, Pennsylvania.

Jane's poetry from that time reveals her heartache, and it wasn't only unrequited love making her unhappy. She

was deeply concerned about the war in Europe, which
had begun a year before, but, away from the sympathetic
environment and friends she had found in Germantown,
few shared her views. After a one-year reunion at Smith, she

wrote to Bob, "I stood alone, except for another
good friend," and the situation was much the
same at home: "I'm learning to keep my mouth
shut. Here in Allentown pacifists are classed
with Communists and Fifth Columnists." While
her position for the next school year was settled,
her heart was not: "With things as they are I
almost wish I weren't tied down to a job, though
it seems a sin to say so," she wrote to Bob. "But
I want to be nearer the heart of the trouble
somehow, not shunted off on a sidetrack with a
lot of contented little girls. It will be my duty to
make them less contented, of course." As painful
and alienating as this discontent often was, Jane embraced it
as a gift, and sought to pass it on.

Even among her family, Jane felt alone. "At meals we have
been doing a deal of talking," she wrote to Bob. "It usually
ends up with me arguing against Father on the subject of
pacifism, until I give up exasperated. We start from opposite
poles, and don't get anywhere. . . . Then Jim breaks in and
asks what is so awful about death anyway, either killing or
being killed. It seems to me that I am trying to explain a
new color or am trying to describe the sea to someone who
has never seen it."

But there was one person who always seemed to understand. Although their ways had parted, Bob and Jane continued by letter the deep conversation that had begun on that unforgettable April evening. It was to Bob that Jane confided her frustrations, joys, questions, and, as the months passed, her poetry as well.

When they could, they saw each other on weekends, and Bob visited the Tyson family at Bay Head in July. During one of those visits they shared a moment which Bob relayed on a scrap found in his papers after his death. It's dated July 20, 1940: "I told thee I wondered, when we first stood there on the jetty, dreaming out to sea, whether I would ever forget those moments of silent oneness. Then as thee turned and looked into me, I knew I never would."

After that, Bob's letter salutations went from a formal "Dear Jane" to "Janie darling— . . . I think of thee so much that thee even gets into the law cases – which is a pretty dull environment, and I hope thee doesn't mind." "I think of thee so much that it is almost like breathing," Jane replied from Lancaster. (The "thees" and "thous" of their speech to one another was a Quaker custom.)

What drew them together? Bob was not the kind of man Jane had imagined as her future husband, and she told him as much. In spite of this there was an ease of communication at the heart of their relationship. What they shared sprang not from a system of dogma or a set of propositions but from what they both loved and cherished.

First, love of life. Jane: "I wonder why some people become tired of life? I don't think I ever could, even through sorrow. . . . It is just that I have yet to feel even a hint of doubt that life is worth living. I think thee has the same assurance; that is possibly one reason we started to watch each other this spring."

Conscience and integrity. Bob: "Sometimes I think how much simpler life would be without a conscience! And perhaps for some it really is. But for me there's a feeling of sureness and calm that comes after one has yielded that makes the struggle unquestionably worth it. . . . Certainly a using of conscience makes us more keenly aware of it, and we could not instantly discard it even if we wanted to – but at the same time a struggle for decision is frequently – perhaps increasingly – difficult." Jane replied: "A conscience is a good thing and a difficult thing. If thee didn't have one as big as a continent, I wouldn't feel as I do about thee."

Sensitivity. Bob: "Perhaps one of the hardest things about trying to live a life that is inwardly sensitive is when a direction comes that, if followed, will hurt or disappoint those for whom we care a great deal. I think this is connected with what I was talking about when we were walking Sunday evening: suffering being inevitable; indeed I think it is necessary, if one is to grow into a depth of understanding and sympathy."

Truth. Jane: "Thee is sure about a number of things, and that I suppose is one reason why I love thee. I'm not sure, myself, yet I feel the need of it. Only why thee cares for me I can't see; certainly it wouldn't be because of my doubt."

Humor. Their letters shine with an ability to laugh at themselves and each other, their jokes often decorated with wicked little smiley faces. Bob: "Now don't be too hard on Fitzy [their nickname for the frosty and exacting headmistress at Shippen School]. I can just picture thee whipping up behind her and yelling BOO! and scaring the poor dear out of (or into) a year's growth of wrinkles." And Jane: "I'm trying desperately not to say anything that you can misinterpret, because I find you hunting for ambiguity and hidden meanings left and right. If it wouldn't have been such a task for my complex brain, I would have used only words of one syllable in this letter. As it is, I hope you have your Webster's handy, so that you can adjust my highfaluting prose into a jargon more compatible with the capacity and inherent handicaps of the Clement cranium."

In September 1940, on the anniversary of their very first encounter, Jane wrote: "A year ago this afternoon I didn't think that I'd be here, or that thee could ever possibly mean so much to me, or that we would have been through so much together by this time. We don't notice the strange way things come about while they are coming about. It is only afterwards that we see the pattern. . . . I trust that thee has found out after a year that I am the college president's daughter, and I hope with all my heart that thee has found me to be a lot more. Chiefly, at this point, I am thine."

That they were in love was clear to both (and to their friends and family), but what they were to do with that love was another question. There followed some difficult months. Jane remembered later, "I had turned away from the established churches. Bob was a truly believing Christian. . . . We wanted to marry, yet Bob felt – quite rightly – that our marriage had to be based on a common faith in Jesus, and I was afraid I might force myself into a faith just for his sake; at the same time I knew (and felt it before he did) that God had led us together, and we were meant for each other." (This is not to say that Bob felt superior. "I am humbled by thy deep searching," he told her, "for if those things come more easily to me, I really don't deserve as much respect as thee . . . and I'm beginning to realize that thy understanding is not only sincere and genuine, but that in many ways it is far beyond mine.")

"Oh darling, we are such fools," Jane wrote to Bob on December 26. "Love is a thing which should be put to work in the world, not kept between two people while they make up their minds. That is one trouble with us – we are spending it all upon each other, in our present arrangement." (She could not have known that she was writing those words exactly one year before their wedding day.)

Two things occurred to move them past this perplexing "present arrangement." First, the escalation of the war in Europe made them realize how easily they could be torn apart. In the spring of 1941, they went through the formalities of wedding preparation in their Quaker meetings so that they could be quickly married if the moment came. In September, they attended a lecture during which Jane realized, suddenly but with complete assurance, that she did believe Jesus was the Son of God, and her Savior. Faith, which she had refused to force, had all but crept up on her. Bob and Jane were formally engaged.

December 7 brought the Japanese bombing of Pearl Harbor. The war, which had loomed on the horizon for years, was at their doorstep. They decided to be married during Christmas vacation. Their wedding was a simple ceremony, held in Jane's family's home, on December 26, 1941.

IT WAS THE SIMPLEST THING

It was the simplest thing that made me see
you did not care a fig for me;
no great denunciation and no thunder
contrived to tear our hearts asunder.

You entered, and I know you saw me there;
by all the stars above I swear
my heart was calling so you must have heard.

Beyond the door a little bird
scratched in the dust as you went out again.
I felt no great, momentous pain.
I watched the door swing to, and heard it latch –
and knew we two were not a match,
and went back to my reading, and forgot
the things we were to be, and now were not.

November 7, 1939
Germantown Friends School
"To R.A.C"

Becca: Jane and Bob were married for over fifty years, so it's refreshing to see that it didn't start with clichés or "love at first sight." It seems like the timing was not quite right when they first met, and Bob couldn't see Jane fully.

The beginning of my relationship with my husband, Nate, was no fairy tale either. When we first met, I was in a relationship. Sometime later, after that relationship had ended, I went on some dates with Nate, but I had a sadness weighing me down, making it hard to see anything clearly beyond my own darkness, including Nate. We called it off. I guess I played the role of Bob in the poem above.

A year or so passed, and a recording project brought us back into the same creative circle. We were making a record at my brother's studio in Winston-Salem, North Carolina. This time, it worked. There was no grand gesture, just a shift in consciousness on both our parts. He was more calm, settled in himself, and I was happier. Most importantly, we could see each other more clearly.

In the poem, Jane makes it sound like Bob initially failed the test of being her match by not noticing her, and she tried to completely let go of the idea of being with him. I find her clear reaction both charming and admirable. I respect her acceptance, and the way she reclaimed her heart in that moment, even if I doubt that she really "forgot the things we were to be, and now were not." (She wrote and saved this poem, after all!)

TO R.A.C. I

I watch the light slip downward to the hills;
the stars swim out of deep and tranquil dusk;
the elm and maple buds are flung about
the world, for yesterday the wind came by;
the hyacinths and tulips pierce the ground,
for yesterday the rain was in the sky.
So brief – so finished – bitterly so near!
For yesterday will never come again,
nor will tomorrow ever be so dear.

April 11, 1940
Germantown Friends School

This and the following poems are from a cycle addressed
"To R.A.C." (Robert Allen Clement), collected and numbered by Jane.

TO R.A.C. IV

My dear, I do not love you as you think,
not half in mirth, nor briefly, but forever.
Grant me some power to mend my imperfections;
admit me strength to make one long endeavor.

I am not all the surface gloss you think;
I have a deep glow, too, if you would see.
I would give proof of faith and fearlessness
if you would only care, and turn to me.

April 16, 1940
Germantown Friends School
"After a week"

TO R.A.C. V

Finis

It's not what happens that decides our end;
it's how the heart takes hold of it and makes
an open wound of pain, or wisdom's scar.
What my heart makes of this, the days will tell.
Therefore return in some safe-distanced year
        to see if I am invalid and lame
or scarred but otherwise quite wise and well.

But do not look to find me quite the same.

April 21, 1940
Chestnut Hill, Pennsylvania

TO R.A.C. VIII

One who has loved is never quite alone,
though all the hills declare our solitude.
Having known you, I am no more afraid,
the essential singleness of blood and bone
when dispossessed, comes never in return;
one who has loved is never quite alone.

May 2, 1940
Chestnut Hill

TO R.A.C. IX

I do not swear I will remember you;
I have sworn that before – and have forgot,
and vowed eternities too many times
to tarnish this with phrases I hold cheap.
I will not even say you are my love;
the word is trite, beribboned, tired with use,
and has grown sickly with the world's abuse.

I say that you are young, when all around
the years are weary, hearts destroy themselves,
and the bright morning of an April day
scarcely moves the dark; and you are clean
when dust of ages blows about the fields
and the new corn is stifled at its birth.
I say that I would choose, if choice were mine,
with all the honesty my heart can give,
to be your fellow out across the hills.

I do not swear I will remember you.
the lines we follow may diverge today
to meet each separate end. But I can say
when I am old, that once the world was true
and I was fearless and was not alone,
and broke the barriers of blood and bone
into the regions of a brighter star;
and when I smell the fragrant dusk of spring
I will be still with joy, remembering
these days no threat, no falsity can mar.

May 4, 1940
Chestnut Hill

TO R.A.C. XI

Look, my love, the mist is on the fields
and westward where the wooded slopes are dark
one star is steadying the falling night;
this is the last hour for the distant thrush;
listen, a church bell tolls beyond the hill:
the valley holds the tokens of the day –
nine strokes – and slowly lets them drift away.
Then thrush and bell and all the trees are still.

Now will you turn and let me speak with you?
What will bear witness to my steadfast love?
How can I say it, show it, make it sure,
then set it free to journey through the world?
I give it up; it would take forever after
to prove in words what only life can show,
and there is too much need of present laughter,
and, in the end, I know that you will know.

June 2, 1940
Bay Head

Becca: This poem captures the essence of the inspired yet shaky uncertainty of new love: the longing to share every experience, to be fully seen, and to know if one's love will be reciprocated.

In the first seven lines of this poem, Jane reminds me of a young girl wanting to share all her favorite things, observations she's always kept to herself, now that she has someone with whom to share her joy.

But then Jane changes the perspective to her questions and thoughts brewing beneath the moment: "Now will you turn and let me speak with you? What will bear witness to my steadfast love?" This stage of new love can be uncomfortable, not knowing if the other person understands how you feel, or how to put your feelings into words.

The last four lines of the poem find resolution, release, and a return to the present moment. Jane realizes the futility of trying to put her love into words – it would take an eternity to explain something that "only life can show." Attempting to explain her love would only distract from life's present joys. Most of all, the end of this poem returns to a strong sense of faith, faith that her heart is true, and that, in time, Bob will know her love.

TO R.A.C. XII

We are tomorrow's past. O love, beware
lest lightly do we build what soon will fall,
and take too freely what is given us,
outstay our welcome with felicity,
and cast our doom on unsuspecting years.

Tomorrow this will be a yesterday;
a circle inwards from the outer tree,
a bit of rain that now has fed the flower.
Therefore, O love, beware lest lightly we
take our brief divinity and fail
and see no further than each other's eye
and then consume and turn to dust and die.

June 14, 1940
Bay Head

THE INLAND HEART

The wind is singing on the sun-struck dunes;
eastward the wind blows, and the level sea
runs with shadows golden-green and dark;
and no gull cries nearby, but far away
where the black finger of the rocks is laid
the white wings flash, the voices flash, and far
across the moving stretch a white sail gleams.

Here I am lost, hedged in with hills and shade;
and the bright music ripples all day long –
thrush and vireo, and in the dark
the harsh cicada; and my soul must fail,
starve for the sudden, final thrust of sea
over the earth's curve, for the steady sun
that now the hills devour when day is done.

July 5, 1940
Pendle Hill, Pennsylvania

THE PATTERNED HEART

The patterned heart is stubborn to reform;
the soul desires forever its first food
and lives but briefly on a different fare;
the eye accustomed to the edge of earth
battles with hills that shut the edge from view;
the ear that listened first to silences
struggles with sound as a bird within the net.

We are not sand to shift beneath the wind,
showing new contours after every storm;
more than the blast of hate must turn my love,
more than the noise of logic change my faith;
my food was peace, my vision space, my sound
the sound of silence, and by these alone
will I be moved to come into my own.

July 5, 1940
Pendle Hill

TO R.A.C. XIII

I will remember you not as you are
but as I willed you were; and you shall move
soft as a shadow in my memory,
returning to the earth again at dark,
springing at sunrise to insistent life.

I will remember you not as you are;
your ghost that walks within my private heaven
will be a lie, and all your fellow-shades
that walk the sweet fields of my single past
shall be as wronged, as erred-upon, as you.

It is an odd thing how the heart is blind
and holds its self-deception like a gem,
an emerald, to gaze through at the world;
I will remember you; but you shall be
a bright-robed falsehood in my memory.

July 6, 1940
Pendle Hill

TO R.A.C. XVI ▶

There are things to be remembered
when the heart is old,
and many words are waiting
before the tale is told;
for many hawks are plunging
upon the summer air,
and still the mice are creeping,
and still the world is fair.

A necessary evil
is portioned to the heart;
we might as well acknowledge
the devil from the start
and know the hasty blossom
as swiftly will decay,
while other flowers are waiting
to grace a forward day.

It is foolish to have wisdom
and folly to be blind;
to see and take and question
must nourish any mind;
reserve a quiet judgment
until the heart is old,
when fewer words are needed
before the tale is told.

September 6, 1940
Lancaster, Pennsylvania

Becca: When I first came across this poem, it jumped off the page as a beautiful song lyric, ideal in length, sentiment, and structure. I saw the first and last stanzas as verses, and the middle stanza as a chorus that follows and informs them both. My song setting (titled "105" after the untitled poem's page number in *No One Can Stem the Tide*) plays into the bitter sweetness of the "necessary evil" Jane speaks of, weaving a dark, yearning texture in the accompaniment, followed by a more hopeful harmony at "and know the hasty blossom," where Jane teaches us that with patience comes love that is graceful and long lasting.

It's hard to believe that Jane wrote this poem when she was twenty-three, still very early on in her relationship with Bob. Her tone here has the deep wisdom and acceptance we see at the tail end of "To R.A.C. XI." This poem offers sage advice from a Yoda-like Jane, speaking on the nature of love as if she's looking back on it at the end of her life.

The "old" heart that Jane speaks of is a wise heart, one that is faithful and true, and carries its truth patiently because it understands that real love is steadfast and enduring.

Sometimes when I sing this song I see the plunging hawks as brave lovers, throwing themselves fearlessly into love, and sometimes I see them as blind and careless creatures. Some-times I see the mice as slow, careful loves, but (even though I don't hate mice) more often I see them as the pests that infiltrate love, nagging us with worry and doubt. But we can't get hung up on this small stuff, and the reason why comes in the following stanza, which I chose as the chorus of this song:

> A necessary evil
> is portioned to the heart;
> we might as well acknowledge
> the devil from the start

The words "necessary evil" are the cornerstone of this poem for me, representing the hardship that is inherent in love, and which we have to accept in order to understand its nature. Including the word "necessary" taps into a harmony of opposing forces, like good and evil, or light and dark, as if to say that you cannot have one without the other. If she had said "evil is portioned to the heart," that would mean something different to me, but "a necessary evil is portioned to the heart" means it's the darkness that makes its opposite more meaningful, just as day has no meaning without the night.

Jane writes, "You might as well acknowledge the devil from the start," reminding us to accept the darkness from the onset because it's part of the nature of life. You don't know the way, you can't possibly. The only thing you can be sure of is that life and love will not be purely joy, or purely sorrow. They aren't meant to be. There is both darkness and light at the root of any experience. By accepting that, you turn a difficult struggle into a graceful dance.

. . . and know the hasty blossom
as swiftly will decay,
while other flowers are waiting
to grace a forward day.

Jane warns that hasty love, love that is rushed or clinging, will not last, while love that is patient and steadfast even through ups and downs or "necessary evils" has the strength to "grace a forward day."

"It is foolish to have wisdom / and folly to be blind . . ." Only fools think they know everything. But it's also foolish to go through life with your eyes closed, skating along the surface, ignoring the truth, and not trying to understand anything.

In the final stanza, Jane draws a path somewhere between these two extremes. Listen, stay open, don't rush to proclaim that you know the answers, but also don't silence your inner wisdom. Meditate, pray, search, learn, and in time, you'll find that your desire to explain your way into knowing is less important than being completely present.

TO R.A.C. XX

The seed of sorrow hides within this flower.
We who have nourished it must take the blame;
we who have turned its earth and given it name
must watch the steady passing of its hour.

But see the yew tree in the winter's cold;
remember now the spruce, the ivy's dark
approach across the snow, the cedar's stark
strong spring of green against a world gone old.

October 21, 1940
Lancaster

TO R.A.C. XXI

Being wrong is being young; the day
that I am right I'll know that I am old.

The night the sea fails to distract my mind;
the hour I am not set adrift by sound
of music; and the moment I am caught
no longer in a web, remembering you,
then I will know that I am old at last.

Being young is being wrong; they say
wisdom is kept exclusively for age.
Yes – but I'll keep my bodkin by my side.
They'll say, so wise was she that – lo – she died.

October 24, 1940
Lancaster
"written in two minutes the night of
Oct. 24th 1940 – exclusively for R.A.C."

AUTUMN SKETCH

The wind in the dry standing corn is the sound of many waters.

(This is the season for remembering,
for gathering in memories like flowers before frost.)

Over the mountains the dark clouds of birds wheel and vanish
and the air stills slowly with the beat of wings
　　in the light no longer.
(This is the season for what is over and done with, finished.
Hold no promise in your hands. Look to the earth no longer,
nor to the sky, for the snows gather.)

The wind through the standing corn is the murmur of many waters;
look for frost on the hillside and milkweed pods
　　smoking along the roads.
(This is the season for remembering;
blow on your hearth's embers, and ask for a little while
no new springing.)

October 30, 1940
Lancaster

TO R.A.C. XXIV

Remembering you, I have no other fear
than that you might forget and have no need
for further knowledge of my growing love;
all else is slight and dim – the broken world,
my soul's division, the uncertain years,
death of a season. These I come to dread
no more; it is your going that I wait,
taut and prepared to wrestle with despair.

Why do I fear? We have no vows to break;
we have our love between us and around
like a bright cloud of music, and the days
sing in their passage when I am with you.
If woe hides deep where joy has placed its claim
and sets the hour to strike across our name,
what use to break this sweet tranquility,
when you have turned to me, and I am you?

November 10, 1940
Lancaster

TO R.A.C. XXV

Sonnet

There is a danger in the length of days,
and quiet hearts are sudden in their end.
I doubt my faithfulness – as slow hours raise
their separate barriers which blur and blend
into the menace of the Inbetween.
No – not my faithfulness, but my hard powers
to keep the memory of what has been
more than a memory in the present's flower.
These days creep round me, circle me, and cry;
and you grow dim, and beautiful, and far:
and I fight through the mists to where should lie
your spirit, waiting, like a cloudless star.
There is a danger when we are apart:
I need your actual hand upon my heart!

December 13, 1940
Lancaster

O stars, yield me a portion of your still
vast reaches that the lovely wind has known;
O hall of night, where quiet walks in peace,
where bright flowers of a slumberous dark have grown,
speak to my heart of patience and release.
Single I stand upon the unsheltered hill.

If love will fail and all my faith must be
unbuttressed and unchampioned; if my soul
must hold itself its own security
and seek alone the hard and perilous goal,
give me – O earth that knows its destiny
unquestioning – the wisdom that the flower
finds when it dies, the knowledge that the hour
gains when the last clear minute ticks away;
yield me admittance, so with secret power,
though lone, I may go downward into day.

December 13, 1940
Lancaster

TO R.A.C. XXVI

There is no returning from this love

(Lo the roads vanish and the warm fields change;
the hills curl round us and the sea is near)

I will be quiet with my destiny.

(Settle upon this hearth, my wayward lad;
plant me a cedar on the sunny slope.)

I will not fear the inevitable claim

(Dusk whispers at the window, the fire leaps;
the sea now holds the quiet reach of dark)

nor the thin brightness of a failing day.

(The voice is gentle and the feet are sure;
the eyes hold laughter and the look of peace.)

For fear will not avail against this love

(the plough will turn the stretches of our sod
and the barns wait the harvest of our needs.)

it is too deep within the heart of God.

Finished April 28, 1941
Lancaster

TO R.A.C.

Where I do travel, there you are,
beside me or before.

By some sweet fortune we were met,
by wisdom's star

were we one instant shone upon
and in the next

unalterably linked and intermeshed.

But it is still astonishment
now I do step

into a strange way lit by faith
tearful yet glad

that there with scarce a word I find
companion body, soul, and mind.

August 1953
Haddonfield, New Jersey

A Welcome to the New BABY

To my daughter

Little one, do not despair
at the snails in your hair...
When I was a child like you
was bothered by them too.

my shoes I would not wear
my knees were scarred or bare
bored me quite like sleep,
the tub seemed very deep

one when you are grown
daughter of your own
walk will you recall
that plagued when

03

Scope for Some Experiment

So leave me scope for some experiment
in finding out just what the good Lord meant
when He created in my patient mother
this untried soul that's me and is no other.

"Response to Criticism"

S EVERAL YEARS AFTER their wedding, Jane and Bob were expecting their first child. Jonathan was born in 1944, followed by Tim in 1946, and then their first daughter, Anne, in 1948. Jane delighted in her children, and enjoyed mastering the art of mothering and home making.

But her life was in no sense confined to the home. As an active member of their local Friends meeting, she became involved in the Spiritual Life Committee, a women's poetry club, and the Women's Problems Group–"What a title!" she would comment forty years later. In 1952, she published a chapbook, *The Heavenly Garden*, with a Quaker press. The poems were written between 1948 and 1952, and several are included at the end of this chapter. But not even the whirl of domestic, social, and literary responsibilities could quiet Jane's discontent. In the midst of all this conscientious "fulfillment," she discovered an aching emptiness.

She writes in the poem "Resolve": "My sins are gentle and refined, / my friends the gentle friends of God; / I must go seek the publicans, / the wild companions of my Lord." The respectable life she and Bob had worked so hard to carve out was not enough. It was not for nothing that Jane had absorbed the stories of God's fools, including George Fox, whose life of unorthodox faith earned him hatred from both church and government authorities. Jane had visions of him walking in on a modern Quaker meeting "and thundering at us," shaking them out of their complacent cycle of conversation and inaction. "Words are a symbol of the mind's defeat," she confesses in one poem—a strange confession for such a talented poet, but not for one who longed for justice, truth, and peace to be realized not in words, but in action.

There was another factor alienating Jane from her milieu. In 1951, at a routine examination two months after the birth of their son Mark, Jane discovered that she was expecting again. It was a difficult pregnancy, and while some of the family's friends gave them a hand in caring for the other children and giving Jane time to rest, others were critical: such a large, messy, "unplanned" family didn't fit the two-kids-and-a-dog-behind-a-picket-fence neighborhood pattern. "I began to put friends and acquaintances into two categories," Jane wrote, "Those who said 'Oh, no! You poor dear!' or something similar when they realized what was happening, and those who said, 'Oh, that is wonderful!'" Their daughter Faith was born in February 1952. It irked Jane to be judged, and to be expected to act, not according to her conscience or faith, but according to restrictive societal norms, which were all too often given a religious gloss. Her poem "Miracle" may well describe her pregnancy with Faith:

> . . . I cannot now communicate
> The lesson that my soul absorbs,
> nor, taught so tenderly of God,
> can I yet translate into words
>
> why what is bondage to the world
> becomes a labor freely done,
> that what I would have called a grief
> is grief and rapture bound in one.

Later that year, an African American family moved into the neighborhood and was met, for the most part, with hostility, even from members of the Quaker meeting. This hostility inspired the Clements and several of their friends to form a "supper club" with this family, regularly eating Sunday dinner together. But there were so many other situations that offended Jane's instincts about justice and truth, which she was helpless to change: an elderly woman was denied membership in their meeting on the grounds that she might "become a burden"; a young Ukrainian war refugee decided to join the air force; a close friend's marriage was destroyed by alcoholism. And all this against the backdrop of smaller frustrations – gossip and backbiting, a judgmental attitude toward poorer members of the meeting – that Jane refused to make peace with, to accept as "part of life."

An answer, or perhaps just the beginning of an answer, came to Bob and Jane and their children from an unlikely place: the land-locked, poverty-stricken, South American nation of Paraguay.

WORDS

I feel the stirring of the unprofitable years,
the weight of prophecy and ancient grief.
We talk, the words flash golden and then die;
the thin smoke curls, beyond the window's dark
a bat cheeps, faint, repeating, in the night.

Words are the symbols of a mind's defeat,
they shape the hollow air with transient life,
and trick and twist and make the spirit reel,
vanish like ember's fire, devour and leave
brave husks and echoes of lost majesties.

September 1940
Lancaster
"after an intellectual discussion on the peace question"

Becca: It sounds like Jane was frustrated that words couldn't do the work of expressing what she knew to be true. In my songwriting, words come slower to me than music. If I'm following my most comfortable way of writing, they come last. I first create a bed of harmonic and rhythmic structure before adding the words, and try to tell a story without them. My music tells the story just as much as the words do.

My favorite music is the kind that pulls on your heartstrings even without the words. I love it when a song creates a space that takes you out of the moment you're in, and just the sound of it makes you feel nostalgia or strength, or whatever it is that the composer has put into that song for you to feel.

As a singer, though, it's really important for me to use words, and I always push myself to use them even when I'm tempted not to. A singer can often speak directly to people's hearts. But that said, I've gone to concerts where the lyrics were in a different language and I still felt the things they were saying, so maybe it's more about the performer or the creator giving her whole self. If you are a sensitive, open-hearted listener, you'll feel it whether the words are there or not.

SONNET

Seeking the fact that lies behind the flower
the soul will break its own mortality;
searching the time that lies beyond the hour
the soul will yield its blind serenity;
that is but briefly to be ill at ease
and then forever to be tranquil-eyed,
stirring the wrath of temporal deities
who hurl pale lightning when they are defied.
The least fine sheaf of millet will repay
the soul's slow contemplation, and the still
ages of starlight between day and day;
the climb is steep to mount a sudden hill;
but if man, fearless, follows stars, he'll find –
lo, he is more than stars, and more than mind.

January 25, 1941
Lancaster

We shall be circled over at length
        by a remoter sky,
and flung into a starrier space
        more deep, more high.

Some day the little mind of man
        will crack and spin
to let the chattering years fly out,
        forever in.

The sea will be more brief to us
        than jewel of rain;
and what now stuns us with its might,
        beauty or pain,

will be as faint as cheep of mouse
        or swing of flower
under the gusty wing of heaven;
        and what seems power

will drop away and pale to dust
        held in the palm;
and what seems passion now will sink
        to leveled calm.

Therefore be quiet with your breath,
        all little men,
and hold some wonder, in the Now
        for the great Then.

May 6, 1941
Lancaster

GULL, AT THE WATER'S EDGE

Gull, at the water's edge
mirrored in shining sand,
sleek in the silver wind
blown from the land;

in the clear fall of dark
past the thin pools of tide
with the gray sanderlings
swift at his side.

Outward beyond the eye
reaches the solitude
out to the end of time
where the winds brood.

One with his element,
quiet, unquestioning,
still, when the spill of wave
scurries the sanderling.

Dusk, and the spell of sea,
tide smell and all the vast
air for his wings when he
rises at last.

October 9, 1943
Ship Bottom, New Jersey

Only the past will yield to poetry;
only the lost years that the wind blows back
out of the stars to mingle with our breath,
so that our tissues take them in again
until they surge once more in human veins
and beat behind our eyes, and know no death.

The present has a substance solid, gross –
clay to be molded, granite to be struck,
passion to flare, and timber piled to burn;
the past is our music, our essential air,
earth of our spirit, deep sea of our mind,
and out of its return we know, we learn.

February 15, 1944
Allentown, Pennsylvania

TO MY UNBORN CHILD

I carry life or death within me;
this little stirring, blind and pushing creature
is the sweet paradox
    inevitable
weighing me down with either joy
    or sorrow.

Teach me, my little one, the slow acceptance,
whether death or life is borne within me.

I am in God's hands, and you
in God's hands
    through me –
all of it God's: the light, the dark,
    the winter,
and this wild, petal-drifting,
    sun-dazed May.

May 13, 1948
Haddonfield

WRITER'S (ABDOMINAL) CRAMP

Maybe Milton tired of his own words
and Keats' own beaded bubbles wearied him,
and Shakespeare's phrases to his ears were bleak,
sounded and resounded from the boards.

How it would comfort me to know they felt
a little nauseated now and then
with their own fare; for I have grown quite ill
with eating of the food my pen does grill.

April 14, 1949
Haddonfield

Becca: I love this poem. I wonder if Jane realized that in writing it, she offers to all of us that same comfort she longed for: that even our artistic heroes struggled with self-criticism.

I've never met an artist who doesn't sometimes get discouraged about his or her art. I'm a slow worker myself, which means I repeat things over a long period of time (ad nauseam) to get them right, and I, too, grow "ill with eating of the food my pen does grill" (tired of the sound of my own voice).

But I've learned that my inner critic is actually a really important part of the creative process. I think Jane must have known this. The themes of self-doubt and self-criticism recur often in her poetry, but she never lets them silence her voice. She knew how to channel even these negative forces into her art.

The trick, for me, is knowing how much power to give my inner critic, and, more importantly, *when*. If you give it an inch at the beginning of the process, it will take a mile. But if you learn how to dance with it a little, it can be a really powerful tool; it can lead you into unexpected inspiration and unexpected choices. It's almost as if you have to make friends with it, so that sometimes you can invite it over for tea, and at other times you can say, "Hey, just wait there for a minute while I finish this, and then we'll talk about it."

If I'm writing a song and that critical voice pops in and says: "This song sounds just like this other song you already wrote,

and *no one* will like it," I try to say: "Oh hey, thanks for coming over! Good to know, I'll write that down, and then once I get this song out of me, I'll come back to that and see what I can do to make that not the case." And then the critical voice can't say anything else at that point.

Whereas if the critical voice says that, and you say, "Oh God, what have I done? Now I'm in trouble," you get into this avalanche of self-doubt that will shut down your art. The worst thing you can do is to fall under that avalanche when you're writing, because the process of creating can be delicate, and it's very easy to get blocked. Knowing that dance is so important: how to keep my focus, tunnel vision, one foot in front of the other, just get the song out, and *then* how to have a romantic dinner with my inner critic afterwards.

JANUARY SONG

Prune when winter is in the bough.
When spring holds sway
then you will say,
I cannot cut it now,
not when the blossoms' sweet
bewitching breath
speaks of the fruit to come,
and not of death.

All future autumns hang
within the seed,
and fruit less fair
will cluster there
if you deny the need
for cutting off, in winter's
numbing cold,
the limbs that will destroy you
when you're old.

January 11, 1950
Haddonfield
"for David"

THE OPTIMISTIC BORE

She is caught in a perpetual June,
the chronic vapidness of blissful weather,
and sees significance ad nauseam
in the least fleeting wing and blowing blossom,
and scatters sunshine everywhere she goes
until one thirsts most avidly for rain
and feels the blacker as she brighter grows
and hopes she will not pass one's way again.

March 1950
Haddonfield

LORD, SHOW ME THYSELF

How unsuspecting do we wait
a visitation of thy power
and heedless wander in a maze
nor reckon up the coming hour.

And when thy finger points at us
we glance behind, confused with doubt
that we are now become the one
thy tutelage has singled out.

This is the moment to deny,
to hide our faces from thy sight,
or else to stand and open wide
the doors of being to thy light.

from The Heavenly Garden
Haddonfield
1948–1952

FOR ONE BEREAVED

Stem and leaf and bud and flower,
growth perceptible each hour
to eyes slow enough to see.

Healing in the shattered bone
until each separate cell has grown
back to weight-bearing constancy.

The heart mends slowly, day by day,
not by man's wit, but in love's way,
rich-laden with the past, yet free.

from The Heavenly Garden

RESOLVE

I'll wash my hands of innocence
and cast the snowy robe aside
and shun the face of purity
to walk where sinners now abide.

The bare and brutal face of hate
I must go forth to look upon
and clasp the hand of treachery
with love as if it were my own.

My sins are inward and refined,
my friends the gentle friends of God;
I must go seek the publicans,
the wild companions of my Lord.

from The Heavenly Garden

LOVE IS THE LAW OF LIFE

Am I deceived, if I have given love
 the voice to spell the essence of my days,
authority to rule in all its ways
and with its urgency my spirit move?
Am I betrayed, in yielding love this power,
in giving it the scepter and the crown,
the brightest banner and the sole renown,
unchallenged victor over every hour?

    It is not I but love who is deceived,
    and love who risks disaster, trusting me,
    and puts its energy in jeopardy
    and will by my defaulting be bereaved.

I have not strength nor majesty to bring
sufficient zeal to such a lord and king.

from The Heavenly Garden

SEA ECHO

If at this juncture I am pressed with sharp
remembering, with the weight of other days,
of sea mist, of the rustling early grass
where little sparrows forage; and the sand
blown in long streamers on the empty road
speaks to me suddenly of other Junes;
and the slow osprey winging out to sea
transports me to that lost shore instantly;
if I am vulnerable to this extent
in these the middle years, with more ahead
presumably than that which lies behind,
how shall I bear the past when I am old?

To garner wisdom is to lose regret;
if that is true I am not wise at all,
standing here weeping for a happy youth,
puzzling over what the past becomes
seen through the lenses of the gathering years.
I must become accustomed to return,
altered myself, to the unaltered scene.
Then if the heart accepts the happiness
of now, not longing for the what-has-been,
the sweet sea echo will not mock, but bless.

from The Heavenly Garden

RESPONSE TO CRITICISM ▶

Do it the way you will – I only know
that it was right for me to do it so.
Take any two right hands and clench them tight,
they will not grasp a rod with equal might –
nor will they be alike when in repose.
Two bushes never bear the selfsame rose.

So leave me scope for some experiment
in finding out just what the good Lord meant
when He created in my patient mother
this untried soul that's me and is no other.

from The Heavenly Garden

Becca: People often approach me with criticism of my art. It is common, after one of my performances, to have an audience member tell me how they would do what I do better. I would venture to guess that scientists and mathematicians deal with fewer folks offering opinions on how their job should be done. But art, being rooted in self-expression rather than in set criteria, has no right or wrong, only varying levels of depth and authenticity. Maybe the artist has studied her craft for decades, drawing from truth or raw personal experience, yet the critic can still claim her art is a failure.

I try to stay open to criticism from others, to hear it and consider it, but not take it personally. Jane's response to criticism is true to form, classy yet direct: "Do it the way you will – I only know / that it was right for me to do it so." She nips the conversation in the bud without being mean or ungrateful. Maybe I'll quote these lines the next time I'm approached by someone who claims to know better than I do how to tell my story.

I would imagine this type of exchange to be even more startling for someone like Jane, who had a very private approach to writing. She wrote for herself, as a means of expression and understanding. Criticizing Jane's writing would truly be like criticizing her "heart's necessities."

The line "Two bushes never bear the selfsame rose" seems to be a nod to art and creativity. Saying "No two roses are the same" is very different from saying "No two bushes bear the same rose." No two artists create the same work of art. When the critic says, "I would do that differently," you can say, "Of course you would, you're a different bush!"

And perhaps my favorite line of the poem: "So leave me scope for some experiment." One of the most important things to me as an artist is freedom of experimentation. Experimentation is the source of creative evolution: without experimentation we'll never fail, and without failure we'll never grow. Jane asks her unnamed critic to leave her room for experimentation in finding her voice and living her life, proud to be her own person, unlike any other.

AT THE SHORE

Out of the black pool of sleep
the broken images like scattered sunlight
merge into morning, and I wake.

Here where the sea beats unangered
the gray gulls waddle along in the gray misty morning
and rise on white wings over the white sea
transformed into grace in their own element.

Must we take lessons always from everything –
gulls fat and ridiculous dabbling their feet in the tide-pool,
gulls flying sublime with the sunlight silver upon them?

Better return to sleep and waken prosaic.
We were meant to both dabble and soar,
and even the loveliest wings get weary.

from The Heavenly Garden

HARVEST

I shall believe in sorrow when it comes
like the first down-wandering of snow,
laying its drift of shadow on my heart,
hugging against the hedges of my soul,
gathering on the lintel of my door.

Its wide and still possession of the air
I shall acknowledge as necessity
and pray and pray, not for an early spring
but for the harvest that the year must bring.

from The Heavenly Garden

MIRACLE

Pity me not. You do not know
the hidden emblem that I bear,
nor the bright crown of circumstance
that all invisible I wear.

I cannot now communicate
the lesson that my soul absorbs,
nor, taught so tenderly of God,
can I yet translate into words

why what is bondage to the world
becomes a labor freely done,
that what I would have called a grief
is grief and rapture bound in one.

from The Heavenly Garden

Now breaks the ice upon the silvered branch,
the brief assault of sun sufficient grace
to crack the cold enchantment and redeem
the straining weighted form. It takes not much

of concentrated radiance to dispel
the sheaths that hold us rigid; one brief glance
of brilliant love will give sufficient heat
to start in frozen heart a tentative beat.

from The Heavenly Garden

ON BEING STIRRED BY AN APRIL SHOWER

A new poem, a new shape,
an ancient thought
now freshly caught
and taught
to rhyme. . .

Why take the time?
Why not live and let
    the moment live?
Why should I give
effort and pain
when April rain
heedless,
    lovely,
        necessary,
is needless of me
or my music?

April 21, 1953
Haddonfield

Landscape with Lapacho Tree

Where is home?

Where willows gather on the crumbling bank
and water rustles in the roots
and swallows skim.
The elm upreaching flings its falling green
the tall pine stands against the west.

Home is not only there.

The pink clad stark flowering tree
across...

The crumbling, heaving th...
the thundering tumult of t...
familiar crisis of the year
the swift blood beating in t...
(but only once, within...
the ice piles ready to d...

The men are knotted by the dam...
the grinding floes rear up and r...
and press and push; and with a sh...
we watch the jam come tumbling out...
(so may we shout, so may we si...
O blessed thaw, O holy spring...

May 1954
Primavera, remembering experiences in...
Northampton

04

The Heart Has Followed
the Curve of the World

Neither is strange,
not now,
when the heart has followed
the curve of the world
to find the same welcome.

"Landscape with Lapacho Tree"

I N THE FALL OF 1952, Jane and several other members
of the Women's Problems Group attended a talk by
Florrie Potts, a prominent Philadelphia Quaker who,
with her husband Tom, had recently visited the Bruderhof.
Also known then as the Society of Brothers, the Bruderhof
was (and still is) a Christian pacifist movement that had
formed in Germany in 1920 in response to the horrors
of World War I and to the terrible inequality of post-war
Europe. In the late 1930s its members were expelled from
Germany for refusing to cooperate with Hitler's regime:
they would not join the military, use the "Heil Hitler"
salute, or accept a Nazi teacher for their school children.
They immigrated to England, but, when World War II broke
out, were forced to move again. By this time, community
members hailed from many European countries – Allied,
Axis, and neutral. That in itself was a witness to the possi-
bility of peace, but it wasn't received kindly by their British
neighbors, as anti-German sentiment rose with the fear of
invasion. The community was again forced to move, this
time to Paraguay.

From Paraguay, the Bruderhof began to send members to North America to raise funds for a hospital they had built to serve their indigenous neighbors. It was through these fundraising efforts that the Potts family first encountered the Bruderhof, and were intrigued enough to visit the community in Paraguay.

The others in the group were interested in Florrie's presentation, but Jane was electrified. "It sounds like heaven!" she told a friend as they drove back to Haddonfield. That December, Tom and Florrie announced their decision to join the Bruderhof: they would soon be leaving their comfortable, honored position among Philadelphia Quakers for the Paraguayan jungle. At this news, the benign interest that many of Jane's friends had felt toward the Bruderhof turned to hostility.

A few months later, hearing that a Bruderhof couple was visiting the Pottses, Jane and Bob decided to pay them a visit. At the Potts's house they met a Bruderhof pastor and his wife, Heini and Annemarie Arnold. "They were completely natural and simple," Jane remembered later, "if a bit thin and worn." She had steeled herself to encounter "a great 'spiritual' personality," but was disarmed by their openness and humility.

During the course of the conversation, it became clear that, once the Pottses left for South America, there would be no North American home base for Bruderhof travelers. Bob and Jane decided to offer their home, and fixed up their attic (the only space available in a small house bursting at the seams with a growing family) as a small guest apartment. If so many children, so close, had earned them their neighbors' disapproval, this new development – the coming and going of bearded strangers in ramshackle cars – earned their scorn and distrust. But Jane was beyond being swayed by their opinions. If anything, it was a relief to no longer play at conformity. The children enjoyed the guests, many of whom were parents traveling away from their families, and adopted them as honorary aunts and uncles.

The year 1953 was full of comings and goings, and decisions to be made. In late summer there was a lull in South American guests. Bob's and Jane's families hoped that they were returning to "normal," but under the appearance of calm was a painful interior struggle. Bob and Jane were both drawn to the Bruderhof. Jane remembered: "What we longed for was a life completely centered around Jesus . . . and that might mean a form of community, but not community for its own sake." The Bruderhof seemed to answer this longing. They were torn, however, between this new attraction and their responsibilities in, and loyalty to, the Society of Friends.

It was a difficult few months. "I am so tired and baffled and feel myself such a hindrance to Bob that I am often in despair," Jane wrote in her journal. "I have felt my own clarity dimmed because of the tenacity of his doubts. I have also felt the gift withdrawn because of my own imperfections and . . . the long interval between my clarity and its being put into practice." The couple's struggle was compounded by their relatives' objections: "Both my family and Bob's mother have been actively upset recently. David and Yvonne [Jane's younger brother and his wife] were here several days and we had long talks with them. They, as agnostics, grasp our intentions and respect the uncompromising attitude more than most 'Christians.'"

The depth of Jane's frustration is clear in her poetry as well:

> Too late we break the siege
> of the close-bastioned heart
> and find the city starved,
> dry to the bone, and dark.

Eventually, Jane and Bob decided that the only way to move past this stalemate of indecision was to visit Paraguay. "Now that the news [of the upcoming trip] has broken, we have had talks with many people," Jane wrote in her journal. "It is a strange feeling to find oneself doing something no one wants one to do. Some are very much disturbed but maintain a steady affection and faith in us. Some are shocked and resentful or horrified."

Bob left in early April, and Jane followed him in early May when Hans-Hermann and Gertrud, a Bruderhof couple whom they had befriended, offered to care for the Clement children for a few weeks. The time in Paraguay was, for Jane, both wonderful and difficult. On the one hand, her attraction to the Bruderhof only deepened: "Perhaps it is like falling in love," she wrote at the time. "One feels deeply in love at first, yet the longer one lives and knows the person the more one loves, and looks back to see how much deeper that love has really grown. . . . We must go forward, not hesitatingly or tentatively, but surely and with faith." But these bright moments had a darker shadow: "My faith that we will reach clarity and unity together becomes submerged in fear that he [Bob] will not be released, and I cannot understand why we have found this cleavage to be so persistent. I feel as if a hand were clamped over my mouth so that I cannot express what I deeply feel either in words or in attitude. . . . Yet God brought us together, and together we must work this through for His sake. But I feel sometimes as if my heart will break."

Just as, at the beginning of their relationship, Bob's slowness and conscientiousness had frustrated Jane, now again, she was ready for a decision long before he was. Since adolescence she had known the feeling of estrangement – for the sake of her convictions – from her family and friends. It was less familiar to Bob. But, only a day after that tormented entry, Jane would return to her journal: "It hardly seems possible it has been less than twenty-four hours since I wrote the last entry, so full of life and redemption has the time been. Bob and I had a period of struggle together that was suddenly broken."

But Jane's journal entries are not only about affairs of the heart. They also describe the people she encountered: "Now that I have visited in many of the homes I am beginning to get a clearer impression of people. . . . They are from all backgrounds and cultures. The only thing they had in common before joining was their dissatisfaction," a discontent that Jane understood fully.

Jane and Bob also witnessed the baptism of four new members, among them Tom and Florrie Potts. "The baptism was the most moving and powerful human event I have ever witnessed or participated in," Jane wrote in her journal, "and one truly felt linked all the way back to Jesus and the early church, as if the apostolic line was really here – and also, since we knew all four, their backgrounds and their journeys, the impact was tremendous. I cannot express what actually happened. . . . What we witnessed was somehow the heart of the Christian mystery. It eludes definition or description: it cannot be grasped once and for all."

Bob and Jane returned to their family in Haddonfield in June, now unified in their decision to wrap up affairs and, once the Bruderhof had established itself in North America, to join them there. In June of 1954, the Bruderhof purchased an old estate in Rifton, New York. Several families moved from Paraguay, and were soon joined by American families hoping to join this new way of life. The Clements visited Woodcrest, the new community, in August, and moved there in September.

Bob and Jane took novitiate vows – promises that signaled a time of discernment – at the community's New Year's Eve service, and, in December 1955, sealed those vows with baptism.

THE CHAIN

Too late we break the siege
of the close-bastioned heart
and find the city starved,
dry to the bone, and dark.

Too late we cut the chain,
who cannot find the key;
the captive soul has died,
the captive flame is quenched.

The devil does not thrust
against the armored gate,
nor counsels us to yield –
he counsels us to wait.

February 2, 1954
Haddonfield
Completed September 19, 1954
Ship Bottom

LANDSCAPE WITH LAPACHO TREE

Where is home?

Where willows gather
on the crumbling banks
and water rustles in the roots
and swallows skim;
the elm up-rushing
flings its falling green;
the still pine stands against the West.

Home is not only these.

The pink cloud of the flowering tree
across the camp
far, in the ridge of woods
struck by the dying sunlight
the lapacho,
and the river parrots
slowly flying
like herons.

Neither is strange,
    not now,
when the heart has followed
the curve of the world
to find the same welcome.

May 29, 1954
Paraguay

FEBRUARY THAW

On the wet bank's rim we stand,
the air wild with the beating rain;
the sodden wood beyond awry
with wild wind from the driven sky:
    (and I know deeply and with pain
    we stand here once and not again.)

The crumbling, heaving thrust of ice,
the thundering tumult of the falls,
familiar crisis of the year,
the swift blood beating in the ear:
    (but only once, within the heart
    the ice piles ready to depart.)

The men are knotted by the dam,
the grinding floes rear up and roar
and press and push; and with a shout
we watch the jam come tumbling out:
    (so may we shout, so may we sing,
    O blessed thaw, O holy spring.)

May 1954
Paraguay

WOODCREST

Who walks beside the hemlocks on this lane,
whose shoulders brush the sumac on the slope
climbing to see the valley flowing out
and the dark folds beyond it, hill on hill?

Upon whose ears does all our music fall?
Whose hand is laid upon our children's heads?
And as the saw bites through the measured wood,
for whose sake do we stand here laboring?

And in the cold with all the world in need,
for whose sake do we open wide the door?
Who lights the fire that gives us energy
and makes of our poor strength His lasting home?

August 1, 1954
Woodcrest, Rifton, New York

GROWTH

At what instant does the summer change?
What subtle chemistry of air
and sunlight on the clean and windsmooth sand?
The small birds at the water's edge –
yesterday they were not there.

So suddenly the magic door is shut,
the trio suddenly is done,
the clasped hands inexplicably apart;
however dear, however bright,
the road we traveled on is gone.

August 12, 1954
Ship Bottom

STRUGGLE

The heart's winter,
the soul's drought,
    the mind's ice
    hardening out,
the deep clutch
of circumstance,
    the numbed spirit
    in a trance –

O break o break

fire in the east,
that we may rise,
    that we may wake!

November 2, 1954
Woodcrest

NOVEMBER RAIN

Now we must look about us. Near at hand
cloud like a fist has closed on all the hills
and by this meager daylight on our land
we see just this, and this, and not beyond.

The sodden trees emerge and stand revealed;
we must acknowledge each one as it is,
stripped and stark, its basic structure clear,
the last leaves fallen, summer's season dead.

And day on day the soft mist softly falls
as the long rain drives across the field
and all the while what we had seen beyond
is lost and shut as if it never were.

And we look closely at each other now,
the bleak roots, black grass, and the muddy road,
the litter that we never cleared away,
the broken flowers from a summer's day –

Oh, stark and clearly we must look within
to weigh at last our purity and sin.

Oh, lovely hills in sunlight far away,
Oh, curving valley where the river sings!
Remembering, we live this discipline,
and hope still beats about us with strong wings.

November 21, 1954
Woodcrest

OUT OF A DIFFICULT AND TROUBLED SEASON

Out of a difficult and troubled season
the timely harvest thrusts amid the stones;
the dry mind that would claim a thousand reasons
melts beneath the Lord's appointed rain.

The furred magnolia buds we bring to warmth
here in the heated room soon bloom and sicken;
the tree without keeps its own secret time.

Powerless are we to move God with our clamor,
to seize the least fringe of His mystery;
but we must wait until the gift is given
and poor, walk faithfully the lanes of heaven.

October 1954–June 1955
Woodcrest

Becca: Jane wrote this poem from the Woodcrest Bruderhof community when she was a few years older than I am now. I was shocked when I found out that Jane was a member of a devout Christian community because I never read her poetry as being inherently focused on religion or Christianity. Every so often I come across a poem like this one, where Jane's faith is apparent, but not in a way that seems exclusive, or that pushes away a non-Christian reader.

This poem demonstrates one of Jane's many poetic strengths: using seasons as a metaphor to illustrate the nuances of our emotional and spiritual struggles. Even after a "difficult and troubled season," the spring somehow finds its way to the sun "amid the stones." I've always been in awe of weeds and blades of grass that poke through the cracks of heavy sidewalk slabs, proving themselves stronger than the heavy burden that weighs down their roots.

The flowers we pick and protect from the elements ("the furred magnolia buds") never last as long as the one left in the earth, keeping "its own secret time." Jane sheds light, through these nature-driven life lessons, on faith and things that I have often struggled to put into words.

The final stanza speaks to religion, as well as life and love. When we fight and scream, take and cling, we come up empty-handed, but life lived with patience, an open heart, and empty hands will be richly blessed.

THE GATE

No one compels you, traveler;
this road or that road, make your choice!
Dust or mud, heat or cold,
fellowship or solitude,
foul weather or a fairer sky,
the choice is yours as you go by.

But here if you would take this path
there is a gate whose latch is love,
whose key is single and which swings
upon the hinge of faithfulness,

and none can mock, who seeks this way
the king we worship shamelessly.
If you would enter, traveler,
into this city fair and wide,
it is forever and you leave
all trappings of the self outside.

April 1955
Woodcrest

Child, though I take your hand
and walk in the snow;
though we follow the track of the mou...
though we try to unlock together the...
of the printed word, and slowly dis...
why two and three make five
always, in an uncertain world--

child, ... I am meant to te...
what is ... in the end,
... together we are
except ... children
meant ... a Father ... unlearn
of th... ult structure
and ... cumbering years
and ...

and you... me and the heav...
to lo...
wit...

given to Pep, April 20, 1965

JTC 14 Aug. 1972 Dorset

Oh shepherd ... the Lord of light
... the far pastures where we stray
through perils + stony way
may Thy voice lead the flock aright

may ... all the lone + scattered sheep
who wander far + heedless roam
through valley dark + hillside steep
hear Thy voice calling, and come
home.

And may we ... to our fold be turned,
all at Thy bidding gathered in,
+ where of old Thy watch fires
burned
may now fires leap + flame again

Oh shepherd ... of light
may ... alone --
... first night

DEC 1969

05

No One Can Stem the Tide

No one can stem the tide; now watch it run
to meet the river pouring to the sea!
And in the meeting tumult what a play
of waves and twinkling water in the sun!

"Manasquan Inlet II"

A S   T H E Y   S E T T L E D into Bruderhof life, Bob and Jane became deeply involved in the life of the community. Bob occasionally taught, and also brought his lawyering skills to bear on the legal and business affairs of the community.

Jane worked as a teacher in the community's grade school, and her dedication is remembered by many of her students. As a teacher, she was famous for being able to calm a rowdy class, often stepping in when other teachers had failed. She never talked down to her students, and they returned her respect. Students remember that Jane rarely raised her voice (one exception being when a boy called Louisa May Alcott's *Little Women* "a silly book"). She passed on her passion for poetry and books of all kinds, reading Tolkien's *Ring* trilogy to her classes when the books first came out. And she passed on her love for the natural world–so evident in her poetry–by taking her students on walks through the woods, during which she taught them to be quiet and attentive to the world around them. Her home and classroom were always full of animals. The family was never without a cat, and there were also mice, chinchillas, snakes, birds, and even Phewie the skunk. Jane became known as an unofficial vet – even if she couldn't heal their sick guinea pig or injured bird, children knew that she would at least do her best.

While Jane poured her creative energy into her students and family (two more sons were born in Woodcrest: Joel in 1957 and Peter in 1961), she continued to write: poems, short stories, plays, musicals, and song lyrics for occasions as the community's unofficial poet laureate. She and her composer friend, Marlys Swinger, collaborated on hundreds of songs: hymns and Christmas carols, children's songs and love songs, to  celebrate the weddings of young friends. Jane also continued to write more personal poetry, but at a much slower pace than before. Her drafts show a poet finding moments for creativity in the midst of a busy life: they are written on the backs of envelopes, grading forms, children's drawings, a note requesting a parent-teacher meeting. Her oldest daughter, Anne, remembers suddenly finding herself alone over the dishes – Mom, suddenly hit by inspiration, had hurried to her room to write it down. Jane quietly tucked away many of her poems without showing anyone, while she used others as personal greetings for friends. Her poem "For Pep" was written for a close friend who lost a child.

In the 1970s, the Clement family moved to England to help found a new Bruderhof community in East Sussex. Although Jane had never lived in England before, or even visited, she quickly felt at home. In a journal entry soon after their arrival, she wrote: "Last night . . . the moonlight was flooding the whole valley, the trees stood out against the silver sky; the beauty of the earth was breath-taking. It is strange to experience a new place where one feels so much at home, as if deep down one has lived here always." Her love of history was rekindled, and she enjoyed taking her students to historical sites during the week and hauling her family to local churches and graveyards on the weekends. She also researched and wrote several short stories that take place in medieval Britain. Some of these were published in a short story collection, *The Sparrow*, later re-issued as *The Secret Flower*.

The Clements eventually returned to the United States, finding a home at a Bruderhof community in Connecticut. In 1980, Jane began a new journal, which she titled "Final Chapter." The theme of patience that runs through so many of her early poems resurfaces, as does a sense of harvest as she looked back on a full life. The journal bears an epigraph taken from scripture: "Be patient therefore, brethren, unto the coming of the Lord. Behold, the husbandman waiteth for the precious fruit of the earth, and hath long patience for it, until he receive the early and latter rain" (James 5:7).

For the most part, the journal is filled with the small events of everyday living – children's marriages, the births and milestones of her grandchildren, the coming and going of friends and neighbors – against the backdrop of world events. Her poem "Guilt" illustrates her insistence that the personal fulfillment she had found would not numb her to a world still full of war and injustice, and "Hope" is dedicated "to the homeless and prisoners":

> Heaven is above me
> no matter where I be:
> in the depths of sorrow,
> in the depths of sea.

Jane continued to teach, and, as each year brought her a new crop of students, she remained dedicated to educating their hearts as well as their minds. Education was never a one-way street. Students and teachers pursued truth together, and this quest demanded, Jane told her journal, "that we are listening, humble, self-effacing, and not defensive."

These were also years of looking back and taking stock of her life. One rainy Sunday in 1984, Jane stumbled across some of her early poems: "I was transported back in time yesterday when I unearthed a collection of poems salvaged from college years in a tattered leather-bound copy book Father once gave to me. What memories they evoked! What a miracle that I am here today and yet how clear it is that I was even then being directed and led in a way I never dreamed!"

WINTER ▶

The dark emerging trees
from the new-winter wood
are lovelier than leaves,
as cold is also good.

The heart's necessities
include the interlude
of frost-constricted peace
on which the sun can brood.

The strong and caustic air
that strikes us to the bone
blows till we see again
the weathered shape of home.

No season of the soul
strips clear the face of God
save cold and frozen wind
upon the frozen sod.

December 1955–June 23, 1956
Woodcrest

Becca: This is the poem that started my relationship with Jane's poetry. You can find the complete story in the Prelude (page *ix*), but in short, I was trying to write a song to honor the life of my friend Kenya Tillery. My early attempts at lyrics were sounding too dark and rooted in my feelings, which was making the song more personal and less universally accessible. For years, the song was like a puzzle that I couldn't crack. Then this poem solved the puzzle. Jane manages to paint the darkness of winter so beautifully, alongside her deep acceptance of its purpose.

Once again, Jane invites us to see the good in seasons of loss and mourning. These "necessary evils" are the "heart's necessities," without which we would not know the sun's warmth or the coming of spring.

The third stanza paints the bitter cold wind that "strikes us to the bone" as an awakening force, shaking us awake and making us see home for what it truly is.

I chose the final stanza as the chorus of my song. Within the context of my song for Kenya, this stanza means that the dark season following loss is the hardest time for the soul, and that nothing breaks down our faith like suffering. But as Jane's first and second stanza suggest, without this frost-constricted interlude we wouldn't be ready for the awakening of the soul when the bright sun comes back. The deeper the loss, the colder the winter, the more beautiful the spring. The devastation and heartbreak of losing someone make you appreciate the people that you still have.

For my song "Tillery" I had written lyrics about springtime first before finding Jane's "Winter" lyrics that finished the story. The spring lyrics were meant to show what we can look forward to after weathering the darker season:

> Dusk settles in later this time of year
> Fireflies; nighttime's chandelier.
> Night'll come as days must end
> But soon the sun will rise again
> Sadness sheds in layers, leading us here
> Springtime's Winter's souvenir
> Winter clothes and Winter fears
> Winter weight is so last year

Jane chorus ("No season of the soul . . .")

> I think what makes Spring so sweet
> Not the roses but beneath
> Is the underlying truth
> that everything must go so soon.

One more Jane chorus here, followed by a joyous repeated refrain to finish the song. This refrain is a setting of two lines of Jane's poem "February Thaw":

So may we shout, so may we sing,
O blessed thaw, O holy spring.

I chose to end my song with this celebratory refrain, repeated
like a mantra reminding us to be grateful for what we have,
and that just as the seasons always change, this too shall pass.

BIRD ON THE BARE BRANCH

Bird on the bare branch,
flinging your frail song
on the bleak air,
tenuous and brave –
like love in a bleak world,
and like love,
pierced
with everlastingness!

O praise
that we too
may be struck through with light,
may shatter the barren cold
with pure melody
and sing
for thy sake
till the hills are lit with love
and the deserts come
to bloom.

1962
Woodcrest

Oh seek – while the hills remain.
God calls, though daylight fails,
the cruel, the pitiful, the proud,
the weak, the brave, the covetous,
the faltering, the wise, the poor,
the kings, the lepers, and the crowd.

Struck through with death, we hold the seed;
life springs, though our pale roots are dry;
though heaven never seemed so high,
God stoops, to touch our need.

And all the ages fall away;
eyes meet, and shoulders touch at last;
Christ waits, and gathers in His day
the present, future, and the past.

1959
Woodcrest

ZACCHAEUS

Zacchaeus in a sycamore
looked upon God, who summoned him;
small man, he had to climb to see,
to forfeit human dignity.

The choice to climb is up or down,
to stretch or stoop, and either way
the self must yield and melt away
if the Lord's face we would see:

Zacchaeus found his tree.

1963
Woodcrest

STORM

When the lions of the sky are roaring,
when wind-eagles high above are soaring,
black horses of the West are thundering on,
and rain like stinging bees is pelting down,

run to the hedges – come – and hide with me.
There we can watch the fury, feel the beat
of some wild weather-anger at our feet
and crouch like frightened rabbit in its form
to wait, unseen, the passing of the storm.

1964
Woodcrest

FOR PEP

Child, though I take your hand
and walk in the snow;
though we follow the track of the mouse together,
though we try to unlock together the mystery
of the printed word, and slowly discover
why two and three make five
always, in an uncertain world –

child, though I am meant to teach you much,
what is it, in the end,
except that together we are
meant to be children
of the same Father
and I must unlearn
all the adult structure
and the cumbering years

and you must teach me
to look at the earth and the heaven
with your fresh wonder.

April 20, 1965
Woodcrest

SUSSEX DECEMBER

The valley hangs in misty rose,
the trees lace black against the sky,
the brief day drowses to a close
and all the birds are still.

But sudden in the West a fire,
under the trees a springing flame,
light level blazing past until
the sun drowns in the hills.

December 1971
Darvell, Robertsbridge, East Sussex

CHRIST THE SHEPHERD

O Shepherd on the hills of light,
in the far pastures where we stray
may thy voice lead the flock aright
through perilous and stony way.

May all the lone and scattered sheep
who wander far and heedless roam
through valley dark and hillside steep
hear thy voice calling, and come home.

And may we to one fold be turned,
all at thy bidding gathered in,
and where of old thy watch fires burned
may new fires leap and flare again.

O Shepherd on the hills of light,
may we acknowledge thee alone
who holds us through the bitterest night
and always, always calls us home.

August 16, 1972
Darvell
"after a trip through the Elan Valley, Wales"

Becca: This poem yearns to be set to music and printed in every hymnal. It's filled with compassion and such a sweet tenderness. Jane's composer friend Marlys recognized this, fortunately, and wrote a setting so their community could sing the words.

In my early teens, I sang in the choir at a church in North Carolina. The choir loft faced a big stained-glass window of Jesus holding a lamb over his shoulders. It was always my favorite window in the church. This depiction comes from a passage in Luke 15, known as the "Parable of the Lost Sheep":

> Then Jesus told them this parable: "Suppose one of you has a hundred sheep and loses one of them. Doesn't he leave the ninety-nine in the open country and go after the lost sheep until he finds it? And when he finds it, he joyfully puts it on his shoulders and goes home. Then he calls his friends and neighbors together and says, 'Rejoice with me; I have found my lost sheep.' I tell you that in the same way there will be more rejoicing in heaven over one sinner who repents than over ninety-nine righteous persons who do not need to repent."

I've always liked the image of Jesus as a shepherd, but the poem's opening line "O Shepherd on the hills of light" takes that age-old imagery to another level.

Jane left her faith as a teenager and then came back to it in a healthier way later in life, but she always stayed so humble. She wrote this poem when she was fifty-five. Reading these words, I picture her a warm, generous woman, deeply honest and selfless. Jane's compassion "for all the lone and scattered sheep" is reflected in the second stanza, as she prays for lost souls to be returned home from the steep, dark places of the mind. The lines about "new fires" make me think of new inspiration of all kinds, not just creative inspiration but also the feeling that burns in everyone, leading us to take on new ventures, to help one another, and to love.

There is so much tenderness in the final stanza, leaving the reader with the feeling that we are wrapped in love and never alone even in the most bitter "season of the soul," and that no matter what, no matter how lost we feel, we can return to this love, this home. This assurance is such a precious gift to be able to carry in one's heart.

THE SPIDER

I watch the spider fling
its most improbable thread –
frail filament
yet steel strong–
from aspen limb to birch
and back again.

So do we fling our faith
from star to star
and under God's eternal, watching care
the perfect orb
will come.

April 1977
Deer Spring, Norfolk, Connecticut

Becca: Jane begins this poem by observing a spider web made of frail filaments that, through its construction, become steel strong. Then halfway through she makes a sudden and unexpected turn to faith, comparing the steps in a journey of faith to the spider's delicate silk, which, under "God's eternal, watching care," weaves a strong, improbable web, a perfect orb. This poem rings especially true, knowing what we do about the way Jane's faith was flung "from star to star."

Jane has a knack for finding pictures of her faith in nature, rich in metaphor and wonder. We can picture this tiny spider working so hard, all alone, weaving an intricate structure strong enough to capture a bug ten times its size.

Jane once wrote in a letter: "Anything worth possessing takes a while to sink into one's marrow. That is true of music too. Anything that is easy is in the end fruitless. Why we are so slow to accept what is hard?"

The spider is never deterred when it's time to build a web. It knows its time and follows through without hesitation, only to take it down again the next morning and then do it all over again. They are nature's lonely artists, whose beautiful sculptures get walked through more often than they are appreciated.

It can be both a struggle and a strength to have a different approach to art than what is "easy." People are often slow to accept something new, so being different, although it sets you apart from the rest of the herd, can also feel like a weakness as it takes the public much longer to come around to "accept what is hard."

It is my nature to create (and enjoy) music that is different from what's "normal." As Jane alludes in her letter, this is not the recipe for overnight success, but like her I have committed to the path less traveled, and I have faith that if I keep "flinging my improbable thread" from branch to branch, I will have a happy and satisfied heart, and a career that is artistically fulfilling.

FOR HEATHER JANE

Little daughter of the stars,
tiny flower in the grass,
scented blossom on the heath,
birdling from the quiet wood,
poppy bright amidst the wheat,
soft little mole from under leaf,
bud with golden secret heart,
garnet hidden in the stone,
wee shining seed that holds a tree:
all these things thou art to me.

God's angels, hover over thee!

June 16, 1978
Deer Spring

LOLLIPOP DAY

This was a lollipop day,
it tasted so good that I licked it away
little by little and lick by lick
as the sun rose high in the blue-and-white sky,
with swallows lining along the wires
getting ready to fly, to fly,
and over the meadows wherever I'd go
I heard crickets madly prestissimo
    in the grass where I'd pass.

When the shadows began to reach out long
and the thrushes had chosen their lullaby song,
I licked and I licked the day away,
slowly I tasted and savored the day.
The lollipop day was almost gone.
The sun slid slowly into the hill.
    One last lick
and I dropped the stick,
    and the day was done.

c. 1983

GUILT

For all man's Palomars,
for all the far-flung gold-consuming dreams
of stepping on the stars,
of pressing out to new eternities;

for all our turning inward to the small
infinitely precious secrets in the blood,
devising ways to alter destinies –
we have forgot the Flood.

We still pluck the Apple,
    we still hide
when God walks in the Garden.

We still turn aside,
while the Child has died.

February 23, 1985
Deer Spring
"on seeing a picture of a starving child"

FERN FIDDLEHEADS

Fern fiddleheads
like a loved story
whose ending we know well
and wait for –

May 21, 1986
Deer Spring

HOPE

Heaven is above me
no matter where I be:
in the depths of sorrow,
in the depths of sea.

In the mines of evil,
in the pits of sin,
Heaven is above me
and the Light creeps in.

Heaven is never sleeping
though my heart is dead,
though my soul is rotten
and all love has fled.

I cannot hide from Heaven,
I cannot hide from Light,
for lo, the Light will seek me
down the streets of Night.

There is no fleeing from it
no matter where I be;
above is always Heaven
and Heaven is finding me.

June 1987
Deer Spring
"for the homeless and prisoners"

Becca: Jane dedicated this poem to homeless and incarcerated people, sending hope and comfort to those who truly need them. It reminds me of Musicambia, a nonprofit organization my husband founded, which brings music lessons, composing, and ensemble performance to prisons, building artistic communities that nurture the humanity of all involved. Here are a few testimonials from incarcerated men who have been students in the Musicambia program at Sing Sing correctional facility:

"We've all become close friends. And people don't have friends [at Sing Sing], not really. Prison is a hard place, but for people who realize that the prison lifestyle isn't something they want to bring back home, the music gives us hope." – Joe

"It's difficult to go back to your cell after a Musicambia day, a day that feels more 'normal' because you can have conversations and express yourself and feel supported and safe. We don't do that anywhere else. Looking forward to Saturdays helps us get through the week." – Jason

"I feel awful when I think about all that I've lost, but it's music that helps to keep me going. It's keeping me sane in an insane world." – Mike

This poem makes me think of the healing power of music and the hope it brings to these incarcerated men, inspiring them to connect with others, to feel proud of what they are doing, and to love themselves. Even in our darkest hours, music finds us and shines a light that guides us out of the darkness.

I N 1996, JANE SHOWED SIGNS of dementia and was diagnosed with Alzheimer's disease, a tragic ending for a woman so gentle and eloquent, to succumb to the inarticulate rage of dementia. Throughout her illness, Bob was faithfully at her side. He was her security when everything else was confusing – and he could sometimes still draw out her old humor and gentleness.

Jane died on March 21, 2000.

In the following weeks and months, her family collected her poetry, discovering some of it for the first time. These were published in *No One Can Stem the Tide: Selected Poems 1931–1991*. The book's title is taken from one of Jane's last poems: "Manasquan Inlet II."

MANASQUAN INLET II

No one can stem the tide; now watch it run
to meet the river pouring to the sea!
And in the meeting tumult what a play
of waves and twinkling water in the sun!

Ordained by powers beyond our ken,
beyond all wisdom, all our trickery,
immutable it comes, it sweeps, it ebbs
and clears the filthiness and froth of men.

1991
Manasquan, New Jersey

Index of Titles and First Lines